fourth edition

W9-BNL-896

power

real estate

letters

LETTERS, E-MAILS, AND MORE TO MEET ALL BUSINESS NEEDS

WILLIAM H.
PIVAR

CORINNE
PIVAR

Dearborn™
Real Estate Education

This publication is designed to provide accurate and authoritative information in regard to the subject matter covered. It is sold with the understanding that the publisher is not engaged in rendering legal, accounting, or other professional service. If legal advice or other expert assistance is required, the services of a competent professional person should be sought.

President: Roy Lipner
Vice-President of Product Development and Publishing: Evan M. Butterfield
Associate Publisher: Louise Benzer
Development Editor: Caitlin Ostrow
Director of Production: Daniel Frey
Typesetter: Todd Bowman
Creative Director: Lucy Jenkins

Copyright 2006 by Dearborn™ Real Estate Education,
a division of Dearborn Financial Publishing, Inc.®

Published by Dearborn™ Real Estate Education,
a division of Dearborn Financial Publishing, Inc.®
30 South Wacker Drive
Chicago, IL 60606-7481
(312) 836-4400
http://www.dearbornRE.com

All rights reserved. The text of this publication, or any part thereof, may not be reproduced in any manner whatsoever without permission in writing from the publisher. All people, properties, corporations, and Web sites are fictional and intended as examples only. Any similarities to people, living or dead, or actual properties, corporations or other commercial entities, or Web sites are strictly coincidental and do not imply endorsement.

Printed in the United States of America.

06 07 08 10 9 8 7 6 5 4

Pivar, William H.
    Power real estate letters / William H. Pivar, Corinne E. Pivar.-- 4th ed.
    p. cm.
    ISBN 1-4195-0473-8
    1. Real estate business--Records and correspondence. I. Pivar, Corinne E. II. Title.
    HD1386.5.P58 2005
    651.7'5--dc22

                                              2005018981

CONTENTS

CHAPTER 3
Solicitations for Expired and For-Sale-by-Owner Listings   43

CHAPTER 4

Responses to Owner Inquiries   59

CHAPTER 5

Residential Buyer Solicitations   71

CHAPTER 6

Land, Business, and Investment Buyer Solicitation   101

CHAPTER 7

Servicing the Listing   119

CHAPTER 8

Buyer Letters   175

CHAPTER 9
Breach of Contract and Other Letters of Conflict   211

CHAPTER 10
Property Management   229

CHAPTER 11
Broker, Lender, and Attorney Letters   259

CHAPTER 12

Personnel Letters   289

CHAPTER 13

Press Releases   315

CHAPTER 14

Miscellaneous Letters   329

INTRODUCTION

In effective communications, personal contact usually ranks first, and telephone conversations come in second. This leaves written communications in third place. Written correspondence does, however, have some distinct advantages over other methods of communication. Besides providing a written record, which allows little room to question the message conveyed, the written word can provide clarity of intent often lost in verbal exchanges. Also at times writing is the only feasible way to communicate effectively because of the recipient's inaccessibility, the sheer volume of people to be contacted, or the complexity of the information to be shared.

The fourth edition of *Power Real Estate Letters* puts fresh, persuasive, concise letters at your fingertips. You can easily adapt them to your own audience. These letters enable you to maximize the benefits of writing and sending real estate letters.

Both new and experienced real estate agents need to use their time effectively, and they must establish and maintain relationships with current and future clients. *Power Real Estate Letters* will save you valuable time and effort in creating letters on hundreds of topics. Using these letters will allow you to reach a large number of potential and current clients. Individual agents and entire real estate offices can increase their productivity by using these letter templates.

Many of these templates include optional or sample information contained in brackets. When several numbered options are supplied, choose one or use your own words to tailor the letter to your specific situation.

Many of the letters can be used as e-mail or fax messages. E-mails and fax messages are effective where you have a relationship with the recipient and time is important as to the delivery of the message and/or its reply.

Legislation You Need to Know

Fax Regulations

The Telephone Consumer Protection Act as well as FCC regulations prohibit sending unsolicited advertisements (junk faxes) to a fax machine. The prohibition applies to both businesses and residences. As of July 1, 2005, permission to send fax advertisements can be granted only with a signed written statement that includes the fax number to which the fax may be sent. This requirement effectively rules out the use of fax messages for real estate solicitation purposes.

E-Mail Regulations

The CAN-SPAM Act of 2003 established national standards for sending commercial e-mail messages. CAN-SPAM is an acronym for Controlling the Assault of Non-Solicited Pornography and Marketing. To protect consumers from being assaulted by misleading unsolicited e-mail messages, unsolicited e-mails must include the following:

- An opt-out mechanism where the recipient can indicate no more e-mails are to be sent

- A functioning return e-mail address

- A valid subject line indicating the message is an advertisement

- The legitimate physical address of the mailer

The CAN-SPAM Act has made it a misdemeanor to send SPAM with falsified header information

National Do-Not-Call Registry

Under the authority of the Telephone Consumer Protection Act, the Federal Communications Commissioner has established a national Do-Not-Call Registry, which applies to interstate and intrastate telemarketing calls. By registering their phone numbers, consumers can be protected from unwanted commercial solicitations. Because the fine for calling someone whose name appears on the Do-Not-Call Registry is up to $11,000 per call, it is important that calls made to sell or lease properties or to offer services be made only after checking the registry.

To find out if a party is on the Do-Not-Call Registry, a broker can request an account number, which can be given to agents. Agents can access the registry on the Internet at *https://www.telemarketing.donotcall.gov*. The registry is by area code.

Following are some important general exceptions to the do-not-call rules:

■ If you have an existing business relationship with a party (18 months after a purchase or sale), you can call that party even if he or she is listed in the registry.

■ After an inquiry, calls may be made to the inquiring party for three months.

■ You may call persons who have given you written permission to call.

■ You may call commercial telephone numbers. (The registry applies only to residential phones.)

■ You may call the numbers on For-Sale-by-Owner ads or signs. A call may be made as a buyer representative but not as a solicitation for seller representation.

■ Calls for purely survey purposes are exempt. However, if any solicitation is included in the call, the call would not be exempt from the do-not-call rules.

For detailed information about the registry and exemptions, you can check *www.fcc.gov/cgb/donotcall.*

> **Because of the National Do-Not-Call Registry, initial buyer and seller solicitations will often be limited to personal contact or letters.**

Which Method Is Best?

This book provides some letters for situations in which personal contact is often the desired method, such as presenting offers, requesting price reduction, or dealing with personnel problems. Consider each situation individually; ask yourself what your goal is and what the best method of communication is for that goal. As long as it is feasible, use the best method, whether that includes letters, e-mails, faxes, personal contact, phone calls, or another method. Also, be sure to comply with the regulations described above.

KISS—Keep It Simple and Sincere

Letters, e-mails, or faxes are simply written messages; as such, they must accurately convey what the writer intends to say. In a written message, the KISS rule applies—*Keep It Simple and Sincere.* In other words, your message should follow these guidelines:

■ Get to the point quickly.

■ Use clear and concise language so that readers will not get a message other than what is intended.

■   Avoid extraneous material that detracts from or obscures the primary message.

■   Be honest.

You may be great at working crossword puzzles because of your extensive vocabulary, but remember that the purpose of your writing is to communicate, not to impress. The most important attribute of any business communication is clarity. It must convey the writer's message to the reader in an unambiguous manner. One of the keys to achieving clarity is brevity. For this reason, the letters in *Power Real Estate Letters* are short and to the point. Short letters are more likely to be fully read and understood by the reader.

Business communications are likely to be read by people who are as protective of their time as you are of yours. Therefore, the message must be quickly understood. If the reader is not getting the importance of the message within the first 15 seconds, chances are that you need to rewrite your message.

Using Sales Letters as Marketing Tools

Sales letters are different from other business letters. A sales letter is really an ad, which is simply a request for business. Real estate sales letters are intended to sell either your services or property. In advertising, the acronym AIDA is often used. It stands for Attention, Interest, Desire, Action. A sales letter should meet these criteria: it should get the reader's attention, generate interest, create a desire for the product (or for more information), and result in either action by the recipient or an anticipation of your call.

When you wish to target a particular party rather than a group, you can make your solicitation letter more likely to be read by sending it as an overnight letter or using a special service such as FedEx. Because it shows that you regard the message as important, the recipient is less likely to discard it without thought.

The letter must grab the reader's attention in the first few sentences. If you have attracted the reader's attention, the entire letter, even an extremely long one, will generally be read. Attention-getting headings can be directed to particular interests of the recipient, or they can even be absurd or humorous statements. The heading must, however, quickly lead to a message of interest; if it doesn't, your solicitation letter will be discarded. Keep in mind that people want benefits, and they must be told quickly that benefits are what you are offering them.

In the real estate profession, you should regard the letter as a tool to get you through a door. Letters don't sell property or services—the sale is up to you.

Testing Your Market

All sales letters are not equally successful. Some letters have phenomenal results, while others fail to generate anything other than mailing expense. Because direct mailing is one of the most costly advertising media in terms of the cost for each contact made, you don't want to waste dollars on mailings that fail to maximize results. Your letter copy is important, and we have provided you with various copy choices for listing and buyer solicitations. However, copy effectiveness will vary regionally and among target audiences. We therefore suggest that you test your market using different copy so that you can concentrate on what works most effectively before any mass mailings are sent.

To evaluate effectiveness you can use different mailing pieces sent to people whose last names begin with different letters. By knowing the number of pieces mailed and the resulting number of appointments, you will be able to track your percentage of success.

Do's and Don'ts of Soliciting by Mail

Here are five do's and three don'ts of soliciting listings or buyers by mail:

Do's

1. *Your mailing should promise a benefit to the recipient.*

2. *Personally address all correspondence.* Never write "To Occupant." Occupants don't buy or sell real estate—people do.

3. *Address each letter to make it look personal to the recipient.* Handwritten is best, but not always practical. The letter should also be personalized by using the recipient's name. With computer aid, this is a relatively simple task.

4. *Target letters to those likely to be interested in your services.* Use mailing lists or reverse directories that will give you the names of residents from their addresses. This rifle approach is better than a shotgun approach, in which much of the shot misses the mark. For example, if your mailing's goal is to locate buyers for lower-cost homes with low down payments, consider mailing to families within the service area that live in moderately priced rental units and mobile homes.

5. *Include your card in every letter.* If your card has a recent photo of you, the card's effectiveness increases; your reader now identifies your name with a particular person. Cards should also include your e-mail address and company Web site.

When targeting a particular individual you should consider a CD-ROM business card. The card, which can be shaped like a normal business card, can be inserted in any CD-ROM drive. The card can contain your current inventory, including virtual tours, a presentation of what benefits your firm offers, and so forth. The card can also include a direct link to your Web site.

Don'ts

1. *Don't use a postage meter, third class mail, a stick-on address label, or a window envelope.* These make it look like junk mail, and junk mail is more likely to be discarded with only a cursory glance.

2. *Don't disguise the purpose of the letter by making your mailing appear to be an official government letter or a check.* Misleading your readers is unethical, and you want to establish yourself as a professional, not a sleazy operator.

3. *Don't use undersized envelopes.* Envelopes that are too small force you to make an awkward fold in the letter.

Testimonials

Testimonials are very effective and can be included as supplements in mailings and e-mails. If the reader can relate to the person giving the testimonial, by being in similar circumstances or from the same area, the effectiveness of the testimonial increases. To obtain testimonials, all you really have to do is ask. Satisfied buyers and sellers usually respond favorably to such a request. See page 172 to find a sample written request for a testimonial letter.

Lists

You will see that some letters in this book contain lists of items identified by a bullet (•) or a check mark (✓). Lists are very effective in sales letters because the reader's eyes are led naturally down the letter.

Color

Color and texture attract attention and can be effectively used in flyers and attachments, but the letters should appear personal. Color makes the letter appear to be a mass-market piece, creating a negative impression when selling real estate. A light color such as buff or gray can, however, convey a professional image. While slick, hard-coated stock can be used for attachments, the letter should be on uncoated stationery.

Follow-Up Calls

Here are four general tips about making follow-up telephone calls to buyer or seller inquiries as well as letter recipients (when you are not precluded from making the call by the Do-Not-Call Registry):

1. *Immediately identify yourself* and tie your call to your letter.

2. *Give minimal information.* The more information you give over the telephone, the less your chance will be of obtaining a face-to-face meeting.

3. *Get information—ask questions.* Answering questions with questions is a good technique to use.

4. *Don't ask for an appointment.* You should set a time and date to meet the prospective buyers or sellers. You will generally want both parties present when you deal with couples. Use an option of two positive choices, instead of giving readers the option of not meeting with you: "Would you [and Mrs. Smith] be available at 4:30 this afternoon, or would 5:00 be more convenient?"

The letters in this book should satisfy more than 90 percent of an average real estate office's written communication needs. The letters in this book are presented in the block style, just one of several styles that could have been used. (We have left blank lines for the date, recipient's name, address, and the signature.) We prefer a pure block style, but others prefer centered dates and signatures. The format is not a significant factor in communication; if you feel more comfortable with another format, please use it.

Have an Idea for a Letter? Contact Us!

If you think there is a need for letters that are not included in this book, please let us know so we can add them in later editions. You may contact us at *pivarfish@msn.com.*

Acknowledgments

The following reviewers provided valuable assistance in the creation of this edition:

Doris S. Barrell, GRI, DREI
Terri Murphy, GRI, CRS, LTG, CREC, Terri Murphy Communications, Inc.
Margaret Nagel, Chicago Association of REALTORS®, REALTORS® Real Estate School
Sylvia C. Shelnutt, Sylvia Shelnutt Training and Seminars
Trish Szego, CRB, CRS, ERA Elite Group, REALTORS®
William R. "Bill" Zales, MA, EdD, Tomlinson Black North Idado Realty Inc.

C H A P T E R

PROMOTING YOURSELF

Letting People Know You Are a Real Estate Agent

LETTER TO FRIEND OR ACQUAINTANCE ON JOINING FIRM

UR
H O M E   R E A L T Y

_____

_____ ←——— *Date and*
                        address
_____

_____

Dear _____:

[1. I am your neighbor at 7318 Elm, the green house on the corner of Elm and Larsen. 2. I am Jeffrey's mother. 3. I enjoyed working with you (on the recent blood drive).]

I have recently joined [UR Home Realty] as a [sales associate]. I am well prepared to meet the real estate needs of all my friends and neighbors.

If you or any of your friends need any real estate services, I would appreciate it if you would think of me.

Sincerely,

_____

Enclosure: ←——— *Card*

NOTE: *This letter is written for a new licensee. Besides your personal friends and neighbors, the letter should go to people you do business with, close friends of family members, parents of your children's friends, members of organizations you belong to, and so on.*

The first paragraph makes certain that the recipient knows whom you are. Your photo on your card will reinforce this reminder.

BROKER LETTER TO NEIGHBORS OF NEW SALESPERSON

UR
H O M E   R E A L T Y

_____ ← _Date and_
_____   _address_
_____
_____

Dear _____:

[Judith Reilly], [your neighbor] who lives [at 111 Midvale Lane in Sunshine Estates], has recently joined our firm as [1. a sales associate 2. an associate broker]. [Judith] has been your neighbor for [four] years. [She] and [her husband] have [two children, Lisa, age nine, and Jeffrey, age seven, both of whom attend Midvale School]. [Judith is a graduate of Ohio State and previously worked in marketing.] [She] has just completed our training program and will be specializing in [residential sales] in [Orchard Ridge]. If you or any of your friends have any real estate needs, we hope you will contact [Judith]. I have enclosed one of [her] new cards.

Sincerely,

_____

Enclosure: ← _Card_

NOTE: _This letter should paint the agent as a person the reader will want to know. It should be mailed over a radius of several blocks around the new employee's home as well as to the employee's special friends and, if the employee has children, to the parents of his or her children's friends. The employee's picture should be on the card enclosed so neighbors who have seen him or her can relate to the employee._

SALESPERSON LETTER TO NEIGHBOR

UR

H O M E   R E A L T Y

_____
_____ ← *Date and*
                       address
_____
_____

Dear _____ :

I am your [1. neighbor 2. new neighbor] at [3752 Elm Drive—the white house on the corner in Sunshine Estates].

I am [1. an associate broker 2. a real estate salesperson 3. a REALTOR-Associate®] with [UR Home Realty]. I wanted you to know that I am prepared to [meet any real estate needs that you might have].

If you or any of your friends have any questions concerning real estate, don't hesitate to call me at [555-1111].

Sincerely,

_____

Enclosure: ◄— *Card*

NOTE: *You could add a handwritten note that says, "I will call you in the next few days to discuss any present or future needs you might have." Don't attach this note if you have not had any recent personal contact with the neighbor and the neighbor is listed on the Do-Not-Call Registry. Enclose your card with your photograph. Your card is more likely to be noticed if you attach it to the letter with a paper clip or staple.*

LETTER TO FRIEND OR ACQUAINTANCE ON DESIGNATION OR COURSE COMPLETION

UR

HOME REALTY

———————— ← *Date and*
———————— *address*
————————
————————

Dear ————————:

[1. Just a short note to let you know that I have been awarded the professional designation (1. CRS 2. GRI) after my name. (1. CRS 2. GRI) stands for (1. Certified Residential Specialist 2. Graduate REALTOR® Institute). To achieve this designation, a REALTOR® must have met the high standards set by the (1. Residential Sales Council 2. National Association of REALTORS®) and must have completed a rigorous course of training.]

[2. Just a short note to let you know that I have recently completed a course in (Financial Skills for the Residential Specialist). This course, sponsored by the (Residential Sales Council), has prepared me to (better advise buyers and sellers in matters such as mortgage choice, tax implications, and available financial alternatives).]

As a result, I am now better prepared to professionally assist buyers and sellers in meeting their real estate needs. Should you or any of your friends be in need of professional real estate services, I hope you will think of me.

[1. Sincerely, 2. Your friend,]

————————————

Enclosure: ← *Card*

NOTE: *If the letter recipient might not immediately identify you from your name, you should include a first sentence such as:* [1. I am your neighbor at 7318 Elm, the green house on the corner of Elm and Larsen. 2. I am Jeffrey's Mother. 3. I enjoyed working with you (on the recent blood drive).]

LETTER TO FRIEND, ACQUAINTANCE, PAST CUSTOMER, AND CLIENT WHEN YOU CHANGE OFFICES

UR
H O M E   R E A L T Y

←— *Date and address*

Dear _____:

Just a note to let you know I am located at a new address. I am now [1. a sales associate 2. an associate broker] with [UR Home Realty] at their office [on Bellflower Boulevard]. I will be able to offer a higher level of service because of the management support and the group of dedicated professionals who work together as a team to fulfill both buyer and seller needs.

[1. I will be contacting you in the next few days to find out if any of your friends need my real estate services. I would appreciate any help that you can provide. 2. If you or any of your friends need real estate services, I would appreciate it if you would think of me.]

Sincerely,

_____

Enclosure: ◄— *Card*

NOTE: *Enclosing a business card with your photo on it greatly enhances your letter's effectiveness; the reader can then place your face with your name. Mail this letter to friends, neighbors, and acquaintances; service people you do business with; members of organizations you belong to (e.g., social, special interest, or religious groups); friends of family members; the parents of your children's friends; previous buyers and sellers you have dealt with; and your active files of prospective buyers and sellers.*

The paragraph indicating you will be contacting the recipient should be used only if you are not precluded from calling by the do-not-call rules.

LETTER TO FRIEND, ACQUAINTANCE, NEIGHBOR, OR FORMER CLIENT UPON OPENING YOUR OWN OFFICE

UR
H O M E   R E A L T Y

_____
_____ ← *Date and address*
_____
_____

Dear _____:

Guess what! I took the big step! No, [1. not marriage 2. I am already married]. I have opened my own office (see letterhead). I am now an independent broker [1. affiliated with (Century 21) 2. doing business as UR Home Realty].

I am very excited about the move. I offer [1. a full range of investment and residential properties 2. specialized service for home buyers and sellers in (West Covina)].

If you are in the area, stop by for coffee and a "Hello"! I could also use your help. I would greatly appreciate any referrals you can provide of friends and neighbors who might be considering buying or selling real estate in [West Covina].

Sincerely,

_____

Enclosure: ◄— *Card*

NOTE: *Asking for help is an excellent approach to use for a person with whom you are acquainted.*

OFFER TO SPEAK

UR

H O M E   R E A L T Y

◄——— *Date and*
         address

Dear _____:

I understand that, like all service organizations, you constantly need speakers. Well, I would like to offer my services.

I have prepared a [30-minute] presentation on [1. the dynamic changes in the Westwood real estate market 2. proposed zoning changes and what they mean to you 3. how the new tax laws will affect our real estate market 4. why real estate investment makes sense in today's economy 5. is there a real estate bubble?] that I think will interest most of your members.

I will be calling you in a few days to discuss my proposal.

Yours truly,

_____

Enclosure: ◄——— *Card*

NOTE: *Your chamber of commerce should be able to give you a list of local service organizations and people to contact.*

LISTING SOLICITATION LETTERS

> **Warning:** It is a violation of federal law to induce people to leave a neighborhood because of fear that values or the quality of life will decline because of changes in race, sex, ancestry, religion, handicap, or familial status in the neighborhood due to new residents moving in.

For specialized mailings, consider the use of mailing lists or the Internet. Use the yellow pages of your phone book under "Mailing Lists" to find lists available in your business area.

If you are mailing a listing solicitation letter to someone who may have already listed his or her home, we recommend adding the following statement to the end of the letter: "If you have already listed your home for sale with another broker, please disregard this letter."

> **Warning:** If a letter is to be followed with a phone solicitation, be aware of federal regulations regarding unsolicited phone calls. Check the Do-Not-Call Registry section in the Introduction.

WE MOVE HOUSES

UR
H O M E   R E A L T Y

_____
_____ ◄—— *Date and
                                  address*
_____
_____

Dear _____:

Did you know that

We Move Houses? (No Size Limit)

We can find a new owner for your home and, if you wish, have you in a new home in record time.

Want to know how we do it? The answer is with a lot of hard work. We develop a marketing plan for a property and then work the plan.

Call me if you wish to know how we would customize a marketing plan for your home. We also offer an electronic comparative market analysis that indicates what you will likely receive from the sale of your home in today's marketplace. This service is provided without any cost or obligation on your part.

If you would like to receive e-mail notification of listings and sales in your area, please contact me by phone or e-mail.

Sincerely,

_____

P.S. If you have already listed your home for sale with another broker, please disregard this letter.

Enclosure: ◄—— *Card*

NOTE: *You could enclose the No-Cost Market Analysis Certificate on page 57 with this letter.*

WANT TO KNOW THE VALUE? #1

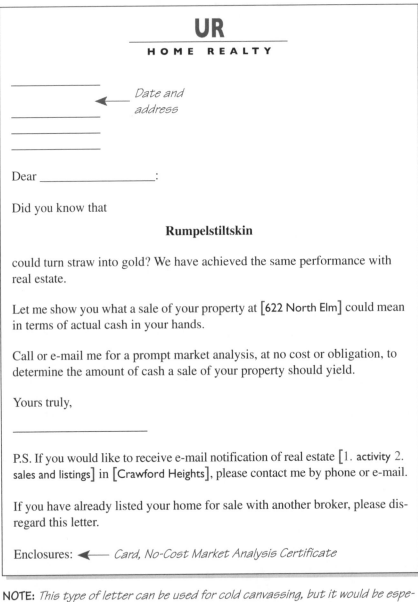

UR
H O M E   R E A L T Y

_____ ◄—— *Date and*
_____   *address*
_____
_____

Dear _____:

Did you know that

Rumpelstiltskin

could turn straw into gold? We have achieved the same performance with real estate.

Let me show you what a sale of your property at [622 North Elm] could mean in terms of actual cash in your hands.

Call or e-mail me for a prompt market analysis, at no cost or obligation, to determine the amount of cash a sale of your property should yield.

Yours truly,

_____

P.S. If you would like to receive e-mail notification of real estate [1. activity 2. sales and listings] in [Crawford Heights], please contact me by phone or e-mail.

If you have already listed your home for sale with another broker, please disregard this letter.

Enclosures: ◄—— *Card, No-Cost Market Analysis Certificate*

NOTE: *This type of letter can be used for cold canvassing, but it would be especially strong if mailed to people who have financial difficulties because of liens, bankruptcy proceedings, foreclosure, divorce, death in the family, criminal action, or automobile repossession. Much of this information is available at your county court house or legal newspapers.*

You might consider enclosing the No-Cost Market Analysis Certificate (see page 57) with this letter.

WANT TO KNOW THE VALUE? #2

UR

H O M E   R E A L T Y

← *Date and address*

Dear _____:

How Much Money Is Locked Up in Your Home?

Because of high demand in [Orchard Ridge], your home has experienced exceptional appreciation. If you wish to explore the possibility of taking advantage of market opportunities, we can supply you with a supported estimate of your home's present market value without any cost or obligation on your part.

If you are interested in knowing the likely market price your home will command, call or e-mail me today.

Yours truly,

_____

P.S. If you would like to receive e-mail notification of listings and sales in your area, please contact me by phone or e-mail.

Enclosure: ← *Card*

ONLY [SEVEN] DAYS TO SELL

<hr>

UR
H O M E   R E A L T Y

_____
_____   ← *Date and*
_____   *address*
_____

Dear _____:

It took

Only [Seven] Days to Sell!

That's right, it took just [seven] days for [UR Home Realty] to sell the home of the [Clarence Jones family] at [2738 West Wilson]. We hope you will welcome your new neighbors, [Henry and Jean Watson]. [They have two children: Lisa, nine, and Henry, Jr., six.]

In the [seven] days it took to sell the [Clarence Jones] house, we actually had several other prospective buyers who would like to live in your neighborhood.

If you or any of your neighbors would like a comparative market analysis that shows you what a home would bring in today's market, we supply this service without any cost or obligation in the hope that when you consider selling, you'll think of [UR Home Realty]. If you want to take advantage of our offer, call me today.

Yours truly,

_____

P.S. If you would like to be kept up to date on listings and sales in your neighborhood by e-mail, please call or e-mail me to be put on our e-mail list.

If you have already listed your home for sale with another broker, please disregard this letter.

Enclosure: ←— *Card*

NOTE: *This mailing should be restricted to the area of a recent neighborhood sale. By providing information that is likely to be of interest and asking the recipient to welcome a new neighbor, you increase the likelihood of the entire letter being read. Do not include personal information about buyers or sellers without their permission.*

You could enclose the No-Cost Market Analysis Certificate on page 57 with this letter.

HOME SOLD—NEIGHBORHOOD SOLICITATION

UR

H O M E   R E A L T Y

_____
                    ← *Date and*
_____   *address*

_____

_____

Dear _____ :

We have just sold the home of your neighbor [Mary Atkins] at [1713 Euclid Avenue]. The new buyers are [Henry and Jean Watson]. [They have three children: Lisa, eight, Henry, Jr., six, and Mary, who is four years old.] I hope you will welcome them to the neighborhood.

In advertising the [Atkins] home, we received a number of inquiries from other families who consider your neighborhood a desirable place to live. We would like to help them but we need homes to sell.

If you or any of your neighbors are considering a move, I would appreciate hearing from you.

Yours truly,

_____

P.S. If you would like to receive e-mails concerning new listings and sales in [Westwood], please contact me by phone or e-mail.

If you have already listed your home for sale with another broker, please disregard this letter.

Enclosure: ◄──── *Card*

NOTE: *Never give out information about a buyer without the buyer's permission.*

FAREWELL TO YOUR OLD NEIGHBORS—
WELCOME TO THE NEW ONES!

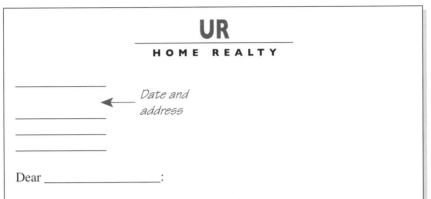

Dear _____:

Farewell to Your Old Neighbors—Welcome to the New Ones!

It must seem that you have said goodbye to many old neighbors; [UR Home Realty] has sold [19] homes in [Truesdale Estates] in the last [six] months. On the bright side, you have the opportunity to make many new friends.

There are good reasons for our phenomenal success in [Truesdale Estates], and I would like the opportunity to discuss them with you.

I would also like to prepare a comparative market analysis that indicates the likely sales price of your home in today's marketplace should you decide to sell. We perform this service without any cost or obligation on your part! If this interests you, please give me a call.

If you would like to receive e-mails concerning the new listings and sales in [Truesdale Estates], let me know by phone or e-mail.

Hoping to be of service,

_____

If you have already listed your home for sale with another broker, please disregard this letter.

Enclosure: ◄— *Card*

A NEIGHBOR LISTED WITH US

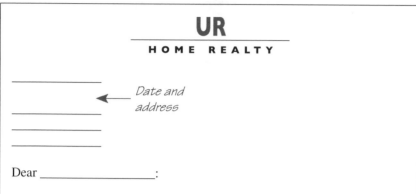

Dear _____:

Do You Want to Know What Your Neighbors Did?

Your neighbors [John and Mary Smith] at [111 Midvale Lane] have just placed their home for sale through [UR Home Realty].

They will be able to take advantage of [1. the exceptional demand our office has been experiencing in your area 2. the current seller's market 3. the rapid appreciation in value of the past few years 4. the recent upturn in the real estate market].

If you want to know what a sale of your home can mean for you in dollars and common sense, I can provide you with a market analysis showing you what you can expect from a sale of your home. This service is provided at no cost or obligation.

[1. I will call you in the next few days to find out if you want to take advantage of this offer and also to ask for your help in choosing a new neighbor. 2. If you want to take advantage of this offer, please call me.]

Yours truly,

_____

P.S. If you would like to be on our e-mail list, receiving notification of new listings and sales in your neighborhood, please visit our Web site at [*www.ur-home.net*].

If you have already listed your home for sale with another broker, please disregard this letter.

Enclosure: ◄——— *Card*

NOTE: *Be sure to obtain permission from the seller before you send this letter. You could include the No-Cost Market Analysis Certificate on page 57 with this letter. Besides soliciting listings, this letter lets neighbors know property is available and it can serve to locate buyers.*

Indicate that you will call only if the neighbor is not listed on the Do-Not-Call Registry.

HELP US FIND A HOME FOR A NEIGHBOR #1

UR
H O M E   R E A L T Y

_____
_____   ← *Date and*
                      address
_____
_____

Dear _____ :

Can You Help a Neighbor?

We need a 3-bedroom home in your neighborhood for a [young family]. [The husband is an engineer and the wife is a schoolteacher. They have an 11-year-old son and a daughter who is 7. They would like to relocate prior to school in September and desire a home within walking distance of Midvale School.]

[1. I will be calling you in a few days to determine 2. Please call me] if you know of anyone in the neighborhood who might consider selling their home to this fine family.

Sincerely,

_____

Enclosure: ◄— *Card*

NOTE: *The heading should get this letter read. The prospective buyers should be real people with whom you are working, and they should be pictured in a very positive manner. People will go out of their way to help specific people, but not people in general.*

This is not only an effective listing canvassing tool, but the effort expended for the buyers you are working for will serve to make them feel indebted to you, reducing the chances of their contacting other agents. Obtain the prospective buyer's permission before sending out this letter.

Indicate that you will be calling only if the addressee is not on the Do-Not-Call Registry.

HELP US FIND A HOME FOR A NEIGHBOR #2

UR

H O M E   R E A L T Y

_____
                    ←———— *Date and*
_____   *address*

_____

_____

Dear _____:

We are seeking a [3-bedroom, 2-bath] home [1. close to 2. within walking distance of 3. within golf-cart distance of] [1. the Midvale Elementary School 2. the Palm Dale Country Club 3. Horton Corp.]. The home is needed for [a young family who has a 9-year-old son and a 7-year-old daughter.] [They are transferring to the area and would like to become members of your country club].

[1. I will be calling you in the next few days to ask for 2. Please call me if there are] any suggestions you can provide in helping us find a home for this fine family.

Yours truly,

_____

Enclosure: ←——— *Card*

NOTE: *You want to picture the buyers you are working with in a very positive fashion. People like to help nice people, especially when they have common interests. This solicitation is extremely effective when mailed to the members of a particular group, such as golf clubs, health clubs, specific companies, and so on. By using your buyer's interests, you can target people within the desired area who have similar interests. Because this solicitation is so effective, you should consider asking prospective buyers if they prefer to live within walking distance of any school, club, or the like. By contacting the group, you should be able to obtain a membership list. A letter such as this also serves to obligate the buyers. Obtain the buyers' permission to send out this letter.*

You may indicate you will call the owners only if they are not on the Do-Not-Call Registry.

WE'RE SOLD OUT!

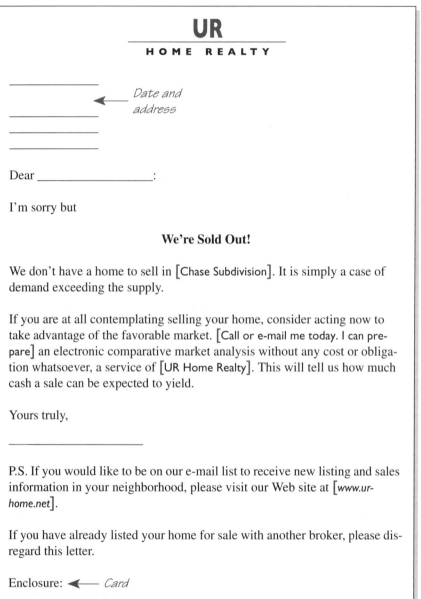

UR

H O M E   R E A L T Y

——————— ← *Date and*
———————   *address*
———————
———————

Dear _____:

I'm sorry but

We're Sold Out!

We don't have a home to sell in [Chase Subdivision]. It is simply a case of demand exceeding the supply.

If you are at all contemplating selling your home, consider acting now to take advantage of the favorable market. [Call or e-mail me today. I can prepare] an electronic comparative market analysis without any cost or obligation whatsoever, a service of [UR Home Realty]. This will tell us how much cash a sale can be expected to yield.

Yours truly,

———————————

P.S. If you would like to be on our e-mail list to receive new listing and sales information in your neighborhood, please visit our Web site at [*www.ur-home.net*].

If you have already listed your home for sale with another broker, please disregard this letter.

Enclosure: ◄—— *Card*

NOTE: *You could enclose the No-Cost Market Analysis Certificate on page 57 with this letter. Before you indicate an unsolicited call will be made, check the Do-Not-Call Registry.*

I APOLOGIZE

UR
H O M E   R E A L T Y

_____
←____ *Date and*
_____   *address*
_____
_____

Dear _____:

I Apologize

If you want to buy a home in [Claridge Estates], I don't really have much to show you. There has been a terrific demand, and the few owners who have taken advantage of the market quickly sold their homes. However, if you really want to buy, call me and I will put your name on my list of buyers, and I will call or e-mail you as soon as properties come on the market.

Now if you are interested in selling, that's a different story! I can prepare for you a report of recent comparable sales indicating the price range we can anticipate from a sale in the current market. This service is at no cost or obligation to you.

Want to take advantage of our offer? Call or e-mail me today.

Yours truly,

_____

P.S. If you would like to be on our e-mail list to receive new listing and sales information in your neighborhood, please sign up on our site, [*www.ur-home.net*].

If you have already listed your home for sale with another broker, please disregard this letter.

Enclosure: ←____ *Card*

NOTE: *You could enclose the No-Cost Market Analysis Certificate on page 57 with this letter.*

AREA ACTIVITY REPORT

UR
H O M E   R E A L T Y

_____

_____   ← *Date and*
                          address
_____

_____

Dear _____:

Your Neighborhood's on the Move!

I thought you might be interested in what's happening around you. During the month of [August], there were [7] sales in [Sunnybrook Acres].

	[Home Information]	[Square Feet]	[Price]
1.	[3BR, 2 Bath, 8 years old]	[1,950]	[$327,000]
2.	_____	_____	_____
3.	_____	_____	_____
4.	_____	_____	_____
5.	_____	_____	_____
6.	_____	_____	_____
7.	_____	_____	_____

If you want to know what to expect from a sale of your home, call for a no-obligation electronic comparative market analysis.

Sincerely,

_____

P.S. If you would like to be on our e-mail list to receive new listing and sales information in your neighborhood, please visit our Web site at [*www.ur-home.net*].

Enclosure: ← *Card*

NOTE: *Don't give out sales information by address unless you have authority to do so. Many sales contracts used by agents allow this information to be disclosed. The Area Activity Report is a good monthly report that will be read. You do not have to have been the sales or listing agent on the properties listed in the report.*

WHAT'S HAPPENING IN YOUR NEIGHBORHOOD?

UR
H O M E   R E A L T Y

_____
_____   ← *Date and*
_____   *address*
_____

Dear _____ :

Do you know what's happening in your neighborhood?

We Are Zeroing In On Your Home!

The following properties have been recently sold
[near your home] [by UR Home Realty].

[3BR Stardust Lane]	[$289,500]
[2BR Stardust Circle]	[$267,500]
[3BR Lynn Court]	[$214,500]
[4BR Lynn Court]	[$374,500]

Would you like to see a "Sold" sign in front of your property as well?

If you would like to be on our e-mail list to receive the latest information on property listings and sales in the area, please visit our Web site at [*www.ur-home.net*]. If you would like to receive a free, no-obligation comparative market analysis indicating what you can expect to receive from a sale of your home, please call me.

Yours truly,

_____

P.S. If you have already listed your home for sale with another broker, please disregard this letter.

Enclosure: ← *Card*

NOTE: *Do not give exact addresses of particular homes without permission of both buyer and seller.*

GENERAL SURVEY LETTER

UR

H O M E   R E A L T Y

_____

_____   ←   *Date and*
                          address

_____

_____

Dear _____:

We would appreciate your help in a survey we are conducting of [the Orchard Ridge Subdivision]. Your assistance will help us in targeting our marketing efforts. Please complete the short questionnaire and return it to us in the enclosed postage-paid envelope.

- How many years have you lived in [Orchard Ridge]? _____

- How many homes have you owned prior to your present residence? _____

- What do you like most about [Orchard Ridge]? _____
  _____

- What do you like least about [Orchard Ridge]? _____
  _____

- Would you recommend your neighborhood to friends seeking to relocate?
  _____ Why? _____
  _____

- Would you like to receive e-mails concerning sales and new listings in [Orchard Ridge]? ❏ Yes (Sales) ❏ Yes (New listings) ❏ No

  Name: _____ E-mail address: _____

Thank you for your help.

_____

Enclosures: ← *Card, postage-paid envelope*

NOTE: *This low-key survey is likely to give you a chance to contact the recipient by e-mail. After providing listing and sales information (with photos), you could offer a no-cost comparative market analysis.*

BUYER/SELLER REFERRAL

_____

UR
H O M E   R E A L T Y

_____
      ◀——— *Date and*
_____   *address*
_____
_____

Dear _____:

Our mutual friend, [Mary Hopkins], suggested that I contact you. As you may know, I [1. found a new home for Mary 2. successfully helped Mary sell her home].

I will be contacting you in the next few days to discuss [1. your real estate needs 2. the marketing of your home].

Yours truly,

_____

Enclosure: ◀——— *Card*

NOTE: *There is some question as to the applicability of the do-not-call rules to referrals. Until we have guidance from the FCC, you should not make telephone contact if the recipient is on the Do-Not-Call Registry. If the recipient is listed on the registry, contact would be personal.*

REFERRAL—THANK YOU

UR
H O M E   R E A L T Y

_____

_____ ◄—— *Date and*
                     address
_____

_____

Dear _____:

We know we have successfully met buyer and seller needs when we get
referrals. I was very happy to receive your referral of [Mr. and Mrs. Jacob
Jones]. I am working with [Mr. and Mrs. Jones] and feel certain I will [1. find
them a new home 2. be able to locate a buyer for their home].

Again, many thanks,

_____

Enclosure: ◄—— *Card*

SORRY I MISSED YOU

NOTE: *This is a door hanger to be left on the front door when no one answers. By perforating the door hanger, the business card can be a detachable part of the hanger.*

BIRTH OF SON OR DAUGHTER
(CONDOMINIUM OR MOBILE HOME OWNER)

UR
H O M E   R E A L T Y

———————
———————   ← *Date and*
address
———————
———————

Dear _____:

Congratulations on the birth of your [1. son, John 2. daughter, Mary-Jane]!
It won't be long before [1. he 2. she] will be running around in seemingly
perpetual motion. You probably will be considering purchasing a home with
your own backyard for [1. John 2. Mary-Jane].

I can help you not only find the perfect home but also sell your [1. condominium 2. mobile home]. Our office provides an electronic comparative
market analysis that indicates what you could expect to receive on a sale of
your [1. condominium 2. mobile home] in today's market. We provide this
service without any cost or obligation on your part! We can also analyze your
finances and explain current lender requirements and loan opportunities.

[Please call or e-mail so I can help you in meeting your real estate needs.]

Yours truly,

———————————

P.S. If you have already listed your home for sale with another broker, please
disregard this letter.

Enclosure: ←— *Card*

NOTE: *From the addresses in birth announcements in local newspapers, you can
ascertain if the parents live in condominiums or mobile homes. These parents are
likely prospects for both a listing and a sale. You could enclose the No-Cost Market Analysis Certificate on page 57 with this letter.*

GRADUATION OF SON OR DAUGHTER

UR
H O M E   R E A L T Y

_____
_____ ←— *Date and*
_____   *address*
_____

Dear _____:

Congratulations! I bet that you feel both proud and glad your [1. son
2. daughter] has graduated from [1. high school 2. college]. Now you will
probably be able to think about your own needs.

Perhaps you want a smaller home, or the low-maintenance lifestyle of an
apartment, condominium, or mobile home. Perhaps you want to retire and
head for a warmer climate. Whatever your housing needs are, I can help you.

Before you make any decisions, you should know exactly where you stand.
I will be happy to furnish you with a comparative market analysis that indicates the present value of your home. In this way, you will know what to
expect if you decide to sell. *Please call me* if you would like this analysis,
offered without any cost or obligation.

Yours truly,

_____

P.S. If you have already listed your home for sale with another broker, please
disregard this letter.

Enclosure: ◄—— *Card*

NOTE: *This letter is most effective when mailed to single parents. This information may be available from graduation announcements. You could enclose the
No-Cost Market Analysis Certificate on page 57 with this letter.*

MARRIAGE OF SON OR DAUGHTER

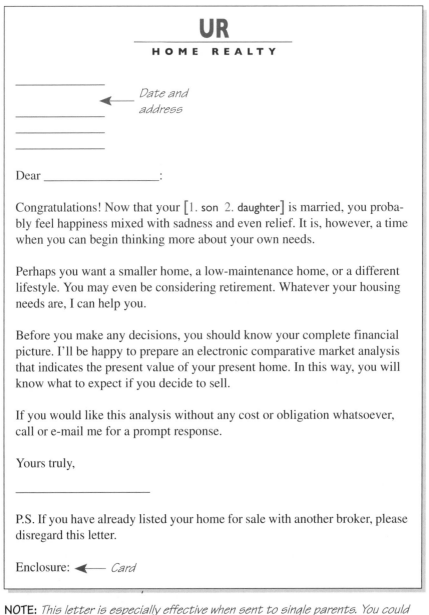

UR
H O M E   R E A L T Y

_____
_____ ◄— *Date and*
_____   *address*
_____

Dear _____:

Congratulations! Now that your [1. son 2. daughter] is married, you probably feel happiness mixed with sadness and even relief. It is, however, a time when you can begin thinking more about your own needs.

Perhaps you want a smaller home, a low-maintenance home, or a different lifestyle. You may even be considering retirement. Whatever your housing needs are, I can help you.

Before you make any decisions, you should know your complete financial picture. I'll be happy to prepare an electronic comparative market analysis that indicates the present value of your present home. In this way, you will know what to expect if you decide to sell.

If you would like this analysis without any cost or obligation whatsoever, call or e-mail me for a prompt response.

Yours truly,

_____

P.S. If you have already listed your home for sale with another broker, please disregard this letter.

Enclosure: ◄— *Card*

NOTE: *This letter is especially effective when sent to single parents. You could enclose the No-Cost Market Analysis Certificate on page 57 with this letter.*
    If there was a photo in the newspaper of bride and/or groom, cut it out and include it with your letter. Use a Post-it® sticker and write, "Thought you might like an extra copy."

RETIREMENT

UR

H O M E   R E A L T Y

_____
_____   ←——— *Date and*
                                address
_____
_____

Dear _____ :

Congratulations on your retirement! I wish you many happy years to enjoy the fruits of your labor.

Many retirees move to areas such as Florida or Arizona for the mild climate, relaxed lifestyle, and the common interests of retirement communities, as well as the lower housing costs. Chances are that you could sell your home, buy a nice home or condominium in Florida or Arizona, and have cash left over to invest in order to supplement your retirement income.

Before you make any decisions, you should first know exactly where you stand. I will be happy to prepare a computer-generated comparative market analysis that indicates the value of your home in the present market. In this way, you will know what to expect if you decide to sell. [1. I will be calling you in the next few days to find out 2. Call me] if you would like to obtain this analysis, offered without any obligation on your part.

Yours truly,

_____

P.S. If you have already listed your home for sale with another broker, please disregard this letter.

Enclosure: ◄——— *Card*

NOTE: *Employee newsletters are an excellent source of retiree information. Some personnel offices also provide this information. You could enclose the No-Cost Market Analysis Certificate on page 57 with this letter.*

Always check the Do-Not-Call Registry before any unsolicited call is made to sell services.

BUILDER SOLICITATION—BUILDING PERMIT

UR
H O M E   R E A L T Y

_____ ← *Date and*
_____   *address*
_____
_____

Dear _____ :

I was pleased to learn that you have taken out a construction permit for another new home at [3476 Poplar Lane]. New construction has greatly enhanced the desirability of the community and has resulted in increased sales activity in the neighborhood.

I believe the most effective new-home marketing effort really starts before construction begins. A plan review by a marketing specialist often reveals that some costly features are not essential, while other features can increase the home's salability and sales price far beyond their additional cost. I will be [1. calling 2. contacting] you in a few days to schedule a meeting so we can discuss ways to ensure a quick sale and to maximize your profits as well.

Yours truly,

_____

Enclosure: ←— *Card*

NOTE: *Send this letter for building permits taken out in the builder's name. Homes being built for a buyer usually have the permit in the buyer's name.*

This letter offers benefits to the reader. Mentioning an impending call encourages the reader to review the plan features, which is a benefit to the builder.

The Do-Not-Call Registry generally does not apply to business phones, but it does apply to residential phones.

OWNER SOLICITATION—BUILDING PERMIT

UR
H O M E   R E A L T Y

_____
_____ ◄— *Date and*
                   address
_____
_____

Dear _____:

I was happy to learn that you have taken out a construction permit for your new home in [Orchard Ridge]. I am certain that you will be happy with your decision, as the area offers exceptional residential benefits.

While it will be some time before you are able to enjoy your new home, it is not too early to consider a marketing plan for your present home at [1812 Thomas Drive].

I would be happy to meet with you to develop a marketing plan for your home that will best meet your needs. While there is absolutely no obligation on your part, I hope that when you see what we can do, you will consider having [UR Home Realty] as your representative.

You may learn more about our services by visiting our Web site at [*www.ur-home.net*].

A call or e-mail can start the marketing process.

Yours truly,

_____

P.S. If you have already listed your home for sale with another agent, please disregard this letter.

Enclosure: ◄— *Card*

NOTE: *When a building permit is taken out in an individual's name and a directory search indicates that the party is living in a single-family home, you can expect the home will be placed on the market.*

LiSTING SOLICITATION—OUT-OF-TOWN OWNER

UR
H O M E   R E A L T Y

_____
_____   ⟵ Date and
                           address
_____
_____

Dear _____:

As you undoubtedly know, owning property that is located far away from you can be challenging. Problems tend to become magnified by distance and often lead to anxiety and frustration.

[1. Right now, we are experiencing an exceptional market. 2. Despite current market conditions, we are selling property.] I believe that we can sell your [three-bedroom home] in [Midvale Heights] at an attractive price. In fact, we would be happy to prepare, without obligation to you, a comparative market analysis to show you what you could expect to receive from a sale in the present market.

[1. I will be calling you in the next few days to ascertain your interests in selling your property. 2. Call me at 1-800-555-1111 if you would like more information about what we can do for you.]

Yours truly,

_____

P.S. If you have already listed your home for sale with another agent, please disregard this letter.

Enclosure: ⟵ Card

NOTE: _The knowledge of an imminent call makes an owner consider the option of selling. Indicate a call if the owner is not on the Do-Not-Call Registry. This letter has greater effect if the property has vacancies, needs repair, or has had recent evictions. You could enclose the No-Cost Market Analysis Certificate on page 57 with this letter._

Having an 800 number increases the likelihood of a call from outside the local telephone area.

OWNERS WHO HAVE HOMES FOR RENT

UR
H O M E   R E A L T Y

_____

_____ ⟵ _Date and_
_____ _address_

_____

Dear _____:

Do You Really Want to Rent Your Property?

Consider these points:

- Do you understand that rental income from a single-family home seldom makes economic sense when compared with the likely sale price?

- Do you understand that when you rent your home, you are placing a tenant in charge of a valuable asset? Consider the dangers of a careless tenant.

- Do you understand that should you decide to sell after you rent the property, your chance of a sale could be diminished because of the tenant's rights?

- Do you understand how lengthy and costly it can be to evict a problem tenant who falsely makes claims such as discrimination, retaliatory eviction, that the property was not in habitable condition, or even claims an ownership interest?

- Do you understand how desirable your home would be considered by many potential buyers?

- Do you understand that the current market conditions offer you an opportunity to realize an amount that could be far greater than you imagined?

(1)

OWNERS WHO HAVE HOMES FOR RENT *(continued)*

(2)

Let us show you how we can sell your home now and what you could expect to receive from a sale. We can furnish market analysis without any cost or obligation on your part.

[1. I will be contacting you in the next few days to discuss the advantages that a sale offers you over renting. 2. Please call me if you would like to know what a sale can do for you.]

Yours truly,

_____

Enclosure: ◄——— *Card*

NOTE: *The paragraph indicating you will be contacting the recipient should only be used if the party is not on the Do-Not-Call Registry. However, if the contact will be personal, and not by phone, you can indicate you will make contact even if the party is on the Do-Not-Call Registry.*

LISTING SOLICITATION—APARTMENTS

UR
H O M E   R E A L T Y

⟵ *Date and address*

Dear _____:

[1. **Tenant Problems?** 2. **Headache Renters?**]

Have you considered the advantage of having your apartment equity in management-free government bonds, tax-free municipals, or . . . ?

- No rents to try to collect!
- No vacancies to worry about!
- No repairs to make!
- No tenant complaints!
- No building inspector problems!
- No evictions!

I will be [1. calling you 2. contacting you] in a few days to determine your interest in selling.

Incidentally, we can perform an electronic comparative market analysis—at no cost or obligation to you—that indicates what you can expect to receive from the sale of your apartment building.

Yours truly,

_____

If you have already listed your property for sale with another broker, please disregard this letter.

Enclosure: ⟵ *Card*

NOTE: *Besides general mailings to owners of apartments, consider checking public records for problem property plagued by evictions, unpaid taxes, code violations, and so on. You could enclose the No-Cost Market Analysis Certificate on page 57 with this letter.*

If you will be calling the owner at his or her residence, make sure the owner is not listed on the Do-Not-Call Registry.

LISTING SOLICITATION—LOT OR LAND #1
(VACANT [1. LOT 2. LAND] LISTING SOLICITATION)

UR
H O M E   R E A L T Y

_____
_____ ←— *Date and*
_____   *address*
_____

Dear _____ :

Is Your Dirt Gathering Dust?

Your [1. lot 2. 20 acres] located on [Dillon Road] is costing you money in

- Taxes

- Opportunity costs in earnings that would be received from investing
  the sale proceeds

Want to Know What Your Dirt Is Worth?

Contact me and I will show you what you could expect to receive in today's
[1. advantageous 2. booming] market.

Yours truly,

_____

Enclosure: ◄—— *Card*

LISTING SOLICITATION—LOT OR LAND #2

UR
H O M E   R E A L T Y

_____

_____ ← *Date and*
                  address
_____

_____

Dear _____:

When Is the Best Time to Sell [1. a **Vacant Lot** 2. **Land**]?

The answer is easy, when there are buyers. Right now we are dealing with buyers who have expressed interest in [1. a lot 2. acreage] such as your [1. lot on Dillon Road 2. 20 acres in Bloomington Township].

If you would like to know what your [1. lot 2. land] should sell for in the current market, please contact me.

Yours truly,

_____

Enclosure: ← *Card*

NOTE: *Never indicate a nonexistent buyer interest.*

SOLICITATIONS FOR EXPIRED AND FOR-SALE-BY-OWNER LISTINGS

EXPIRED LISTING #1

UR

H O M E   R E A L T Y

_____
_____   ←—— *Date and*
_____   *address*
_____
_____

Dear _____:

I [1. showed your home while it was listed with (Kenco Realty) 2. toured your home when it was first listed with (Kenco Realty)].

I have some suggestions that I believe will help in selling your home. If you would contact me, I will be happy to go over my ideas for a successful sale.

Yours truly,

_____

P.S. If you have again listed your home with another agent, please disregard this letter.

Enclosure: ◄—— *Card*

NOTE: *Ideas for selling could be in preparing the house to show in a better manner, a redirection of advertising, price adjustment, and so forth.*

EXPIRED LISTING #2

UR

H O M E   R E A L T Y

_____

_____ ◄—— *Date and*

_____   *address*

_____

Dear _____:

[Considering market activity, I was surprised that your home failed to sell while it was listed for sale.]

Did you know that the three most common reasons a home fails to sell are:

1.   Failure to target the marketing toward the most likely buyer

2.   Improper pricing

3.   A negative first impression (which in many cases could be corrected with minimum expenditure)

I would like to offer my experience at no cost or obligation to you. I will analyze your home and give you my recommendations in writing as to how your home can be sold.

[1. If you are interested in having a no cost or obligation analysis as to why your home failed to sell, please contact me. 2. I will stop by to see if you are interested in having a no cost or obligation analysis of why your home failed to sell.]

Yours truly,

_____

P.S. If you have already listed your home for sale with another broker, please disregard this letter.

Enclosure: ◄—— *Card*

NOTE: *When you meet with the owners, go over all of prior agents' communications with the owners to ascertain how the agents' activities were directed.*

FOR-SALE-BY-OWNER LISTING #1

UR
H O M E   R E A L T Y

_____   ← *Date and*
_____   *address*
_____
_____

Dear _____:

Can You Pass the Owner's Quiz?

- Do you have a buyer?
- Have you qualified him or her on financial ability?
- Is your buyer contractually obligated to the purchase?
- Has your buyer been able to arrange the necessary financing?

If all the answers are yes, then congratulations on your sale! If you answered no to any of these questions, you have not yet sold your home.

I will be calling on you to find out how you scored and to show you how [UR Home Realty] can sell your home without any cost to you.

Yours truly,

_____

Enclosure: ◄— *Card*

NOTE: *"Without any cost to you" would be explained in that your fee actually comes out of the buyer's pocket. It is part of the buyer's price. Buyers understand that it is their money that pays brokerage fees, and when buying direct from an owner they expect the price to be reduced by the amount of the fee.*

Use reverse directories to obtain owners' names from addresses or telephone numbers. You can also locate an owner from the office of your tax assessor or your local title company. Never address a letter "To Occupant"!

FOR-SALE-BY-OWNER LISTING #2

UR
H O M E   R E A L T Y

_____
_____ ⟵ *Date and address*
_____
_____

Dear _____:

If I had a full-price buyer for your home, would you be willing to pay our fee? Please call me if the answer is "Yes"!

Yours truly,

_____

Enclosure: ⟵ *Card*

NOTE: *This short note will generally result in owner interest. It provides a chance to be invited to view the premises and to talk to the owner. While you have not said you have a buyer, you only asked if the owner would pay a fee if you had one. Chances are you will be working with several potential buyers who might be interested in the home. Agreeing to pay a fee to a particular buyer is just one step away from agreeing to pay a fee for any buyer.*

   This letter can be used for expired listings as well as For-Sale-by-Owner listings.

FOR-SALE-BY-OWNER LISTING #3

UR
H O M E   R E A L T Y

_____   ← *Date and*
_____   *address*
_____
_____

Dear _____:

I believe your home at [1821 High Street] will meet the needs of a [young family] that I [am working with] in their search for a new home. [They have a son, age 11, and a daughter, age 9,] and particularly desire [a Colonial home within the Wilson School District] such as your home.

[1. Please call me 2. I will be stopping by] so that we can discuss their needs and to ascertain if your home is likely to be of interest to them.

Yours truly,

_____

Enclosure: ◄— *Card*

NOTE: *Always use a real family you are working with who are likely to be interested in the house. The owners will likely try to sell you on their house and will be receptive to a short-term listing to accommodate your particular buyer. If your buyer is not interested in the house, the owners will generally be more receptive to a longer term exclusive listing than they would have been had they not signed a listing with you already.*

If you are acting as a buyer agent and will not be attempting seller representation, then you may call the owner even if listed on the Do-Not-Call Registry. You can call to arrange to show the home but not to solicit business.

FOR-SALE-BY-OWNER LISTING #4

UR

H O M E   R E A L T Y

Date and
address

Dear _____ :

Why Do For-Sale-by-Owner Signs Get Replaced by Agent Signs?
Because Agents Sell!

Utilizing a real estate agent means the following:

- You are protected against unscrupulous buyers hoping to pay less than market value for your home.
- No unescorted, unqualified persons will enter your home.
- Contracts are likely to end in a sale—not in a courtroom.
- You are able to meet buyer financing needs.
- You are no longer a prisoner in your own home waiting for the bell to ring.
- You are more likely to sell your home.
- The sale will likely result in higher net proceeds.

Please think about it. I will stop by your home at [2 P.M. this coming Saturday] to answer any of your questions and to prove that everything I have told you is true. If this time is not convenient, please call me so I can arrange a more convenient time.

Yours truly,

_____

Enclosure: ◄—— _Card_

NOTE: _The approach that the owners can expect you at their door at a particular time forces the owners to consider your message. It can also result in a telephone contact initiated by the owners. While this approach is not for every salesperson and might result in some antagonistic owners, some agents have used it very effectively where owners are on the Do-Not-Call Registry._

FOR-SALE-BY-OWNER LISTING #5

UR
H O M E   R E A L T Y

_____
_____ ⟵ *Date and*
                    address
_____
_____

Dear _____:

You probably know that

No Agent = No Commission

That seems like a good reason to try to sell without an agent, except "no agent" all too often means "no sale." That explains why agent signs replace so many For-Sale-by-Owner signs.

I will call on you at [2 P.M. this coming Saturday] to show you not only the positive benefits I can offer but also the dangers of owner sales. If I can show you how I can put more money in your pockets, will you want to talk with me?

Looking forward to seeing you,

_____

Enclosure: ⟵ *Card*

NOTE: *Telling owners you will be coming to their home is a strong approach that might create a negative reaction in some owners.*

When you call on owners, reference your letter and ask, "Would it be all right if I took a look at your home?" or, "Would you be offended if I asked to take a look at your home?" This type of an approach will likely give you an opportunity to tour the property and comment about positive features.

FOR-SALE-BY-OWNER LISTING #6

UR
H O M E   R E A L T Y

_____

_____ ← *Date and address*

_____

_____

Dear _____:

Can You Use Some Free Help?

Our office supplies [1. purchase offer forms 2. For-Sale-by-Owner suggestions] to owners who wish to sell their homes without the use of an agent. We do so without cost or obligation. We also provide a free estimate of value based on current documented sales.

No, we are not a charity—we do this hoping that if you later decide to use an agent's services, you will remember our assistance.

Please call to set up an appointment so I can drop off the forms and explain how to use them and to answer any questions you might have.

Yours truly,

_____

Enclosure: ◄— *Card*

NOTE: *The free offer is an effective door-opener. By explaining how the forms are to be filled out, with appropriate warnings, mandatory disclosures, applications for financing, qualifying ratios, FICO scores, and so on, the owner will begin to understand that selling a home is more complicated than just finding a buyer. You should then be in a position to discuss the benefits of having professional representation.*

FOR-SALE-BY-OWNER LISTING #7

UR
H O M E   R E A L T Y

Date and
address

Dear _____:

SOLD!

Is this the sign in front of your home? Or is it simply

For-Sale-by-Owner?

The likelihood of turning the second sign into the first sign is very slim, which explains why broker's signs replace so many For-Sale-by-Owner signs.

Facts:

1. Most calls on For-Sale-by-Owner signs come from people who can't afford the home they are calling about.

2. Most calls from newspaper ads are from people who would not be satisfied with a home priced in the range they inquired about.

Without having a variety of homes to match inquiries, most of an owner's efforts end up wasted and precious days will be lost.

I will contact you in the next few days, not to try to saddle you with agent selling fees but to show you how I can help you have more money in your pocket after a sale.

Isn't what you actually net more important than anything else?

Yours truly,

_____

Enclosure: *Card*

FOR-SALE-BY-OWNER LISTING #8

UR
H O M E   R E A L T Y

_____   ← *Date and*
_____   *address*
_____
_____

Dear _____:

Are you

Selling Without an Agent?

You Can Do It, but BE CAREFUL!

I have enclosed a group of helpful hints and warnings that we have compiled to help owners who don't wish to use an agent. Study them carefully. Not only can they mean the difference between a sale and no sale, they can also protect you against a lawsuit or losing your home to an unscrupulous buyer.

If you want an explanation of any of this material or would like to know how you could benefit financially and emotionally from being represented by an agent, please contact me.

I will check with you in a few days to see how you are doing and to offer whatever advice I can.

Yours truly,

_____

Enclosure: ← *"How To Sell Without an Agent" can be adapted as an enclosure (see page 54).*

NOTE: *Weekend afternoons are a good time to contact FSBO owners who are trying to sell their homes because they are often at home hoping a buyer will contact them.*

HOW TO SELL WITHOUT AN AGENT

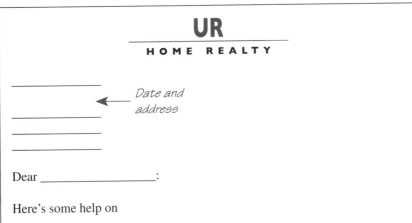

Dear _____:

Here's some help on

How to Sell Your Home Without an Agent

1. **Change ads regularly.** Ads lose their effectiveness if repeated without change. Three days is plenty for one ad. Rewrite ads to appeal to different categories of likely buyers. Use plenty of adjectives. Spend time writing good copy because your ad competes with many ads for similar property.

2. **Obtain purchase contract forms.** [Call our office if you do not have any.] Complete the purchase contract except for date, price, terms, and signatures. Make certain that you fully understand every provision. If a prospective buyer wants to use his or her own contract, be alert. Take it to an attorney. What might appear to be a standard form could be one-sided and not say what it appears to say at first reading. With desktop publishing, many wheeler-dealers are using their own forms where the small print taketh away what the large print giveth!

3. **Check financing at least once a week with a mortgage company so you will be able to help a buyer understand his or her down payment and monthly costs for various types of mortgages tailored to the buyer's needs.** Be prepared to explain loan types to prospective buyers. Many excellent texts are available to help you. You should also understand front-end and back-end qualifying ratios and FICO scores. If you don't understand them, you could waste days, weeks, or even months of effort on a buyer who is unable to obtain financing because of existing debt, insufficient income, or prior credit problems.

(1)

HOW TO SELL WITHOUT AN AGENT *(continued)*

(2)

4. **If a prospective buyer uses the words "subordinate" or "subordination" in the offer, turn and run.** If you sign, no matter how good it looks, you are likely giving away your home to a sharp operator. Also, be alert for any deals that seem too good to be true—they generally are. Be particularly wary with any buyer who is buying without any of his or her own cash. If the buyer ends up with more cash than he or she started with, you can be certain you are the victim of a scam. Television infomercials feature buyers who brag about paying practically nothing to own valuable property. A number of fast-talking seminar promoters have instructed thousands in unethical and often illegal procedures. Offers of mortgages on other property, notes, colored stones, diamonds (especially uncut), or other claimed valuables should send you running to an attorney. If you don't have one, I would be happy to recommend several. When an agent is involved, the fast operators don't waste their time. That's why they love For Sale by Owners.

5. **Be certain that you have considered and fully understand the effects of the following:** seller discount points, payoff penalties on existing loans, assumability of loans, ownership of the impound account, and all closing costs. You should also understand the dangers of "subject-to" financing as opposed to loan assumptions.

6. **Make certain that you are prepared with all seller disclosures mandated by state law.** If you are not prepared, you may not be able to obligate a buyer to a sale; and if you fail to make a proper disclosure, you could be inviting a lawsuit and substantial damages.

7. **Make certain that you fully understand the requirements of state and federal fair housing legislation,** or you could find yourself paying a fine or a penalty.

8. **Make certain you know who a prospective buyer is before he or she crosses your threshold.** There have been far too many horror cases of trusting homeowners who open their homes to persons with intentions other than buying and treat them as if they were honored guests. Try not to be alone when prospective buyers visit.

9. **Beware of contingent offers.** As a result of a contingency, the property could be tied up for months or even years. The buyer could be a dealer who wants to hold the property as if it were an option that would be exercised only if another buyer is located.

HOW TO SELL WITHOUT AN AGENT *(continued)*

(3)

10. **Price it right.** How did you arrive at your price? Unless you have a written comparative market analysis that considers all recent sales of comparable property, your price could be merely a hunch. Too high a price will almost certainly guarantee that your property will not be sold, and you will be simply wasting time and effort. Too low a price will mean you are giving away dollars that are rightfully yours. You want a realistic price that gives you an advantage over your competition in creating interest in your property. You should then hold to your price with only minor concessions.

11. **Understand fully the tax consequences of the sale.** How much, if any, of the sales price will be subject to taxation, and at what rate? [Have you considered the tax benefit of providing some seller financing on an installment sale?]

If you are determined to sell your home yourself, we wish you good luck. I will, however, [1. be contacting you in the next few days 2. look forward to your call] to discuss some of the advantages of having agency representation that you may not have considered.

Yours truly,

_____

Enclosure: ◀—— *Card*

NOTE: *This letter can also be adapted as a handout or as an enclosure with other For-Sale-by-Owner letters. Even though the letter is long, it will be read, because it appears to be offering benefits.*

NO-COST MARKET ANALYSIS CERTIFICATE

Free Market Analysis

This certificate is good for one free electronic comparative market analysis indicating the likely sales price you could expect to receive for your home in today's marketplace.

This analysis is provided without any charge or obligation on your part to list or sell your home.

[Bob Jones]   [555-8200]
[UR Home Realty]   Evenings: [555-6173]

NOTE: *This certificate can be mailed to For-Sale-by-Owner families as well as to potential clients in general. It can also be used as an enclosure or flyer.*

UNSUCCESSFUL LISTING ATTEMPT

UR

H O M E   R E A L T Y

———————— ◄——— *Date and*
———————— *address*
————————
————————

Dear _____:

Thank you very much for the opportunity to visit your home in [Westwood].
I believe that [UR Home Realty] can help you find the perfect family who
will appreciate all your home has to offer.

I will be contacting you again in a few weeks to give you an update on market conditions to help you analyze your marketing efforts and to choose a
plan for success.

Yours truly,

————————————

Enclosure: ◄——— *Card*

NOTE: *A good time for a personal follow-up contact is late in the afternoon when the owner has had an open house.*

RESPONSES TO OWNER INQUIRIES

Owner inquiries that can lead to listings should elicit a priority response. If a face-to-face or phone response is not practical, you should consider an e-mail or a fax response. There will be times when a party can be reached only by letter or desires a letter response. In such cases consider an overnight delivery service such as FedEx.

Many of these letters can be used for an e-mail or a fax response. If so used, you should clearly indicate in the subject that you are supplying information that was requested.

RESPONSE TO VALUE INQUIRY #1

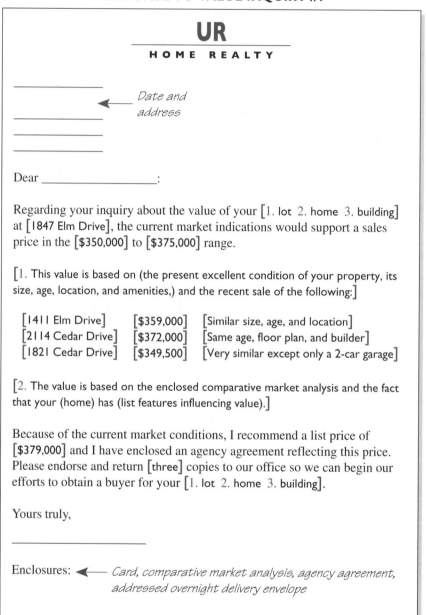

UR

H O M E   R E A L T Y

——————————— ← *Date and*
———————————   *address*
———————————
———————————

Dear _____:

Regarding your inquiry about the value of your [1. lot 2. home 3. building] at [1847 Elm Drive], the current market indications would support a sales price in the [$350,000] to [$375,000] range.

[1. This value is based on (the present excellent condition of your property, its size, age, location, and amenities,) and the recent sale of the following:]

[1411 Elm Drive]   [$359,000]   [Similar size, age, and location]
[2114 Cedar Drive]   [$372,000]   [Same age, floor plan, and builder]
[1821 Cedar Drive]   [$349,500]   [Very similar except only a 2-car garage]

[2. The value is based on the enclosed comparative market analysis and the fact that your (home) has (list features influencing value).]

Because of the current market conditions, I recommend a list price of [$379,000] and I have enclosed an agency agreement reflecting this price. Please endorse and return [three] copies to our office so we can begin our efforts to obtain a buyer for your [1. lot 2. home 3. building].

Yours truly,

———————————————

Enclosures: ← *Card, comparative market analysis, agency agreement, addressed overnight delivery envelope*

NOTE: *Do not give out information concerning sales without the permission of buyers and sellers.*
Never give a value estimate without carefully checking the property and recent comparable sales.

The positive features should show that you appreciate the property's benefits. Don't be picky about the negative features, but list some of them when you are certain that the owner realizes they are present.

Whenever you want the recipient to mail an enclosure back to you, include a self-addressed envelope, preferably using a prepaid, overnight service.

The last paragraph assumes that the owner will list the property. By reading this assumption and the instructions, owners often comply.

If possible, the letter should be followed by a phone call to ascertain if the owner has any questions.

Because the owner contacted you, the do-not-call rules do not apply.

RESPONSE TO VALUE INQUIRY #2

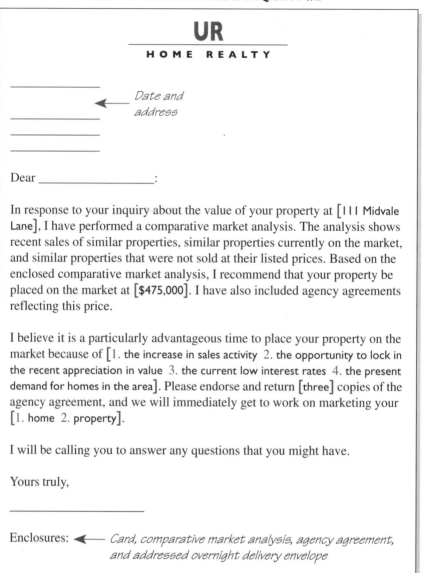

UR

H O M E   R E A L T Y

_____   ← *Date and*
_____   *address*
_____
_____

Dear _____:

In response to your inquiry about the value of your property at [111 Midvale Lane], I have performed a comparative market analysis. The analysis shows recent sales of similar properties, similar properties currently on the market, and similar properties that were not sold at their listed prices. Based on the enclosed comparative market analysis, I recommend that your property be placed on the market at [$475,000]. I have also included agency agreements reflecting this price.

I believe it is a particularly advantageous time to place your property on the market because of [1. the increase in sales activity 2. the opportunity to lock in the recent appreciation in value 3. the current low interest rates 4. the present demand for homes in the area]. Please endorse and return [three] copies of the agency agreement, and we will immediately get to work on marketing your [1. home 2. property].

I will be calling you to answer any questions that you might have.

Yours truly,

_____

Enclosures: ← *Card, comparative market analysis, agency agreement,*
                    and addressed overnight delivery envelope

NOTE: *The term "agency agreement" has a benefit connotation. "Listing" often has a negative connotation because the word is associated with commission rather than with benefits. See notes in previous letter.*

RESPONSE TO VALUE INQUIRY #3

UR

H O M E   R E A L T Y

_____
_____   ← *Date and*
                  address
_____

_____

Dear _____ :

You wanted to know what you should be able to net from a sale after paying off your loan and all sales-related expenses.

The answer is [$146,000] cash. That is our current best estimate of what you will have after paying off the mortgage and all sales and closing costs for a sale of your home at [28146 Hampton Road].

This estimate is based on the enclosed comparative market analysis indicating that your home should sell for [$349,000]. The enclosed seller's proceeds estimate shows the estimated deductions from the gross sales price to arrive at the net.

I have also enclosed agency agreements reflecting the [$349,000] sale price. If [$146,000] cash interests you, please endorse and return [three] copies of the agreements to our office so we can immediately get to work on selling your home [and take advantage of this favorable market].

I will be calling you to answer any questions that you might have.

Yours truly,

_____

Enclosures: ◄——— *Card, comparative market analysis,*
                   seller's proceeds estimate, agency agreement,
                   and addressed overnight delivery envelope

NOTE: *Like the prior two letters, a value inquiry should be answered by mail only when the owner is not available for a personal presentation.*

RESPONSE TO VALUE INQUIRY—
POOR MARKET CONDITIONS

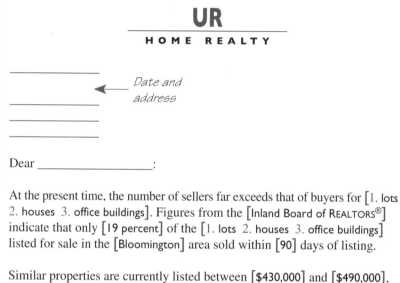

UR

H O M E   R E A L T Y

Date and
address

Dear _____:

At the present time, the number of sellers far exceeds that of buyers for [1. lots 2. houses 3. office buildings]. Figures from the [Inland Board of REALTORS®] indicate that only [19 percent] of the [1. lots 2. houses 3. office buildings] listed for sale in the [Bloomington] area sold within [90] days of listing.

Similar properties are currently listed between [$430,000] and [$490,000], but they are not generating much buyer interest at these prices. When properties have sold, the sale prices have generally been significantly lower than the prices at which properties were listed. The enclosed comparative market analysis confirms this. This does not mean that we cannot sell your [home at 3817 Midvale Circle]. In fact, I am optimistic as to its salability, provided we give your [home] a competitive edge. A list price of [$409,000], which you can see is in line with the actual sale prices of similar [homes], will attract buyer attention and is likely to result in a sale even under our present market conditions.

I have enclosed an agency agreement for your property reflecting the above price. Please endorse and return [three] copies. I will be calling you in a few days to answer any questions that you might have.

Yours truly,

_____

Enclosures: ◄—— *Comparative market analysis, agency agreement,*
and addressed overnight delivery envelope

NOTE: *When most listings expire unsold, this letter's strength is its honesty. It will be a salable listing if you get it—not one likely to cost you money.*

RESPONSE TO VALUE INQUIRY—REPAIRS NEEDED

UR

H O M E   R E A L T Y

_____
_____ ← _Date and_
_____   _address_
_____

Dear _____:

I have carefully examined your home at [381 Lemon Court]. The resulting comparative market analysis is enclosed.

While I am confident that I will be able to find a buyer at the price indicated in my analysis, you should seriously consider some property repairs.

The work I recommend consists of the following:

1. [Paint exterior.]

2. [Repair porch and railing.]

3. [Paint entry way, living room, and kitchen light colors.]

4. [Install new lighting fixture in kitchen.]

5. [Replace floor tile in bath.]

6. [Professionally clean carpets.]

Based on [1. an enclosed estimate from Harkin Home Maintenance 2. my experience in handling similar repair work], the total cost should be about [$2,500].

From the comparative market analysis, you will see that these repairs should result in an increase of [$5,500] in the selling price.

I would be happy to assist you in obtaining firm bids for all the work and also to assist you in securing any desired financing.

(1)

RESPONSE TO VALUE INQUIRY—REPAIRS NEEDED *(continued)*

(2)

I have enclosed an agency agreement for the property based on selling the property without any repairs. Please endorse and return [three] copies. If you decide to go ahead with the repairs and improvements, we can adjust the price to reflect the improvements.

I will be calling you to answer any questions that you might have.

Yours truly,

_____

Enclosures: ◄—— *Comparative market analysis, estimates, agency agreement, addressed overnight delivery envelope*

NOTE: *The choice is not whether to endorse a listing or not, but whether to make repairs or sell the property "as is."*

Again, a letter such as this should be used only when a personal presentation is not possible.

VALUE INQUIRY—APARTMENT
LISTING AND MANAGEMENT

UR
H O M E   R E A L T Y

———————————
←———— *Date and*
———————————   *address*
———————————
———————————

Dear _____:

I have completed an in-depth analysis of your apartment building at [11476 Jackson Street]. The enclosed comparative market analysis is based on the following:

1. [Raising the rents of units one, three, and seven an additional $40 per month and raising the rents of units four, six, eight, and ten $20 per month. These rents are currently below market rents for comparable (Eastside) units.]

2. [Painting vacant units five and nine as well as replacing carpeting.]

3. [Painting entry hall and replacing all carpeting in public areas.]

4. [Painting the exterior and performing needed landscaping work, including planting flowers.]

We would be happy to take charge of all required work. Enclosed is a property management agreement as well as an agency agreement. Please endorse and return [three] copies of each so that we can immediately start preparing your property for a favorable sale.

I will contact you within the next few days to answer any questions that you might have.

Yours truly,

_____

Enclosures: ←——— *Comparative market analysis, property management agreement, agency agreement, addressed overnight return envelope*

NOTE: *When you sell apartments, having management authority will allow you to make the property more salable and increase your likelihood of success.*

ABOUT OUR FIRM

UR
H O M E   R E A L T Y

_____
_____   ◄─── *Date and*
                                address
_____
_____

Dear _____ :

In answer to your inquiry about [UR Home Realty], I would like to tell you about our firm.

[We have served the real estate needs in (Anderson County) for (26 years).]
[I have been engaged in the real estate business since (1970).] [1. We are one of the largest firms in the area, with (56) salespeople in (three) offices. 2. We are a small firm specializing in (suburban residential property).]

[As a member in good standing of the (Pineview) Multiple Listing Service, we are able to make your home available to (118) offices and more than (600) salespeople. Our success record has been exemplary over the past few years and (based on the present market,) I expect continued success for the future.]

For more information about [UR Home Realty as well as testimonial letters from buyers and sellers], I hope you will check our Web site: [*www.ur-home.net*].

I have enclosed a comparative market analysis prepared for your home, showing what you could expect to receive at a sale. Also enclosed is an agency agreement reflecting our recommended sale price. Please sign and return [three] copies of the agreement to us.

I will be calling you to answer any questions you may have.

Yours truly,

_____

Enclosures: ◄─── *Comparative market analysis, agency agreement,*
                 addressed overnight return envelope

NOTE: *Personal contact is always preferable to a letter.*

REFERRAL OF INQUIRY

UR

H O M E   R E A L T Y

_____
_____ ⟵ *Date and*
_____   *address*
_____
_____

Dear _____ :

I appreciate your considering [UR Home Realty] for marketing your property at [48141 Calhoun Road].

Because [1. we limit our activity to Sun City 2. we do not handle commercial property 3. we do not have a property management department], I have referred your inquiry to [Lynn Jones] at [Jones Realty]. [Lynn (1. devotes her efforts to the Mayville area 2. specializes in commercial property 3. specializes in property management and has the prestigious Certified Property Manager (CPM) designation).] [Lynn] will be contacting you in the next few days.

[1. We have successfully referred (1. buyers and sellers 2. persons in need of property management) to (Lynn Jones) in the past and feel certain that (she) will be able to help you. 2. (Jones Realty) is a member of (Refer-All, Inc.), the referral service to which we belong. Because the members are all trained professionals, I feel certain that they will be able to help you.]

Again, thank you for considering [UR Home Realty]. If we can serve you in the future, please feel free to contact me at [555-1111].

Yours truly,

_____

Enclosure: ⟵ *Card*

NOTE: *This letter treats a value inquiry as an offer of a listing. It increases the likelihood that the referral firm will be able to obtain an agency agreement.*

REFUSAL OF OPEN LISTING

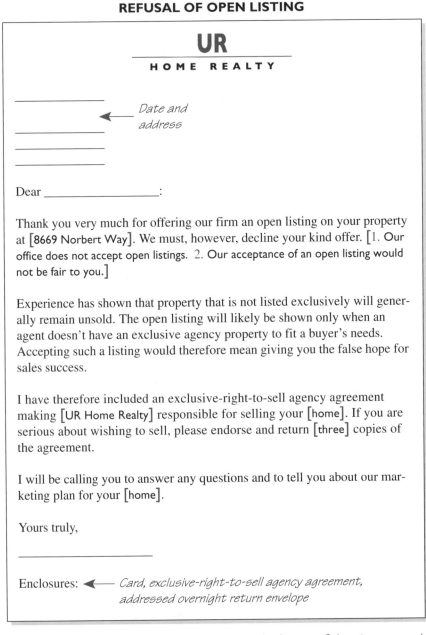

UR
H O M E   R E A L T Y

_____

_____   ← *Date and*
                                address
_____

_____

Dear _____ :

Thank you very much for offering our firm an open listing on your property at [8669 Norbert Way]. We must, however, decline your kind offer. [1. Our office does not accept open listings. 2. Our acceptance of an open listing would not be fair to you.]

Experience has shown that property that is not listed exclusively will generally remain unsold. The open listing will likely be shown only when an agent doesn't have an exclusive agency property to fit a buyer's needs. Accepting such a listing would therefore mean giving you the false hope for sales success.

I have therefore included an exclusive-right-to-sell agency agreement making [UR Home Realty] responsible for selling your [home]. If you are serious about wishing to sell, please endorse and return [three] copies of the agreement.

I will be calling you to answer any questions and to tell you about our marketing plan for your [home].

Yours truly,

_____

Enclosures: ◄— *Card, exclusive-right-to-sell agency agreement,*
              addressed overnight return envelope

NOTE: *This letter is for an owner who lives outside the area. Otherwise personal contact should be made. You may also wish to include a comparative market analysis. To many, the term "agency agreement" creates an image of a helpful partnership, while the word "listing" carries a more negative connotation.*

RESIDENTIAL BUYER SOLICITATIONS

LETTER TO RENTER #1

UR

H O M E   R E A L T Y

_____
◄—— *Date and*
_____   *address*
_____
_____

Dear _____:

Tired of Renting?

- Would you like to enjoy the privacy of your own home?
- Would you like affordable home payments?
- Would you like home equity rather than rent receipts?

Do you want to find out how you can be an owner—rather than a renter—with a down payment and monthly payments tailored to your individual needs?

Call me at [400-7610] now for a no-obligation homebuyer analysis that can mean an end to rent receipts.

Yours truly,

_____

Enclosure: ◄—— *Card*

NOTE: *This letter, as well as others in this section, is directed toward turning tenants into owners. For mailings, we suggest using a reverse directory to target apartment dwellers. Letters to units that have many younger families will be especially productive.*

An additional enclosure can be a sheet showing photos of several homes without any information other than a statement such as "No down payment needed" or "5% down will make it yours."

LETTER TO RENTER #2

UR
H O M E   R E A L T Y

_____
_____   ◄——— *Date and*
                                  address
_____
_____

Dear _____:

Want to

Escape the Landlord?

If you're tired of collecting rent receipts and would like to have something for your money, I have homes for you with the following amenities:

- Very low or even no down payment
- Monthly payments similar to rent
- Three and even four bedrooms
- Your own [double] garage
- Your own [fenced] backyard

Call [400-7610] today and say goodbye to your landlord.

Yours truly,

_____

Enclosure: ◄——— *Card*

NOTE: *This letter, as well as others in this section, is directed toward turning tenants into owners. For mailings, we suggest using a reverse directory to target apartment dwellers. Letters to units that have many younger families will be especially productive.*

An additional enclosure can be a sheet showing photos of several homes without any information other than a statement such as "No down payment needed" or "5% down will make it yours."

LETTER TO RENTER #3

UR
H O M E   R E A L T Y

——————— ← *Date and*
———————   *address*
———————
———————

Dear _____:

Do you

Love Your Landlord?

I bet your landlord loves you. Your landlord gets the rent and tax deductions, and you get rent receipts. That's a pretty good deal—for your landlord.

Kiss Your Landlord Goodbye

A low-down-payment or even a no-down-payment loan can put you in your own home by [Labor Day]. What you have to do is call [400-7610].

Yours truly,

_____

Enclosure: ◄——— *Card*

NOTE: *See note on prior letter.*

TENANT SOLICITATION

_____ **UR** _____

H O M E   R E A L T Y

_____
_____ ← *Date and address*
_____
_____

Dear _____:

Before we advertise to the general public, we would like to give you the first opportunity to purchase the home at [8847 Highland, the white house just down the street from where you are renting]. It has just been placed on the market.

Call me now at [400-7610] for additional information and to discuss various possible financing arrangements. Incidentally, we also have some other very interesting properties available.

Yours truly,

_____

Enclosures: ◄— *Card, photograph*

NOTE: *This letter gives very little information, but it makes the tenant think of the possibility of becoming an owner.*
If the home has good curb appeal, include a color photo.

OFFER TO QUALIFY FOR A LOAN

UR
H O M E   R E A L T Y

_____
_____   ← *Date and*
_____   *address*
_____

Dear _____ :

Can You Afford to Buy a Home?

With current low interest rates, chances are that you can not only become a homeowner, but you may likely qualify for a much finer home than you believed possible.

Free Loan Qualifying Analysis

Allow me to prepare, at no cost or obligation to you, a homebuyer qualifying analysis. This analysis will show you how much you can afford to finance under a variety of available loans, including some having no down payments and very low down payments. To obtain this personal home purchase qualifying analysis, all you have to do is call [400-7610].

Yours truly,

_____

Enclosure: ◄— *Card*

NOTE: *This is an excellent approach for young families who are currently renters.*

BUYER MONTHLY COSTS ESTIMATE WORKSHEET

UR
H O M E   R E A L T Y

←— *Date and*
address

Dear _____:

I have prepared the following estimate of the true monthly costs of home ownership, considering the tax benefits offered by home ownership.

The estimate is based on the following assumptions:

Purchase price	[$295,000]
Total closing costs	[$4,000]
Down payment	[$60,000]
Amount to be financed	[$239,000]

[30-year fixed rate] loan at [6%] interest

Estimated Gross Monthly Costs

Principal and interest	[$1,432.92]
Property tax	[$375.00]
Homeowner insurance	[$42.00]
Other [Association Dues]	[$60.00]
Total estimated monthly gross costs	[$1,909.92]

Tax Benefits (Monthly)

Estimated deductible interest	[$1,195.00]
Estimated deductible property tax	[$375.00]
Monthly total tax deductions	[$1,570.00]
Estimated tax bracket (federal + state)	[37%]
[$1,570] × [37%] = monthly tax benefit	[$580.90]

(1)

BUYER MONTHLY COSTS ESTIMATE WORKSHEET *(continued)*

(2)

Estimated Net Monthly Costs

Estimated gross monthly cost   [$1,909.92]

Estimated monthly tax benefits   [$580.90]

Monthly cost adjusted for tax benefits   [$1,329.02]

Although these costs are estimates only, I have tried to be as realistic as possible, and I believe that actual costs will not vary significantly from this estimate.

I will call you in a few days to discuss the estimate [and to arrange some showings of homes that I believe will interest you].

Yours truly,

_____

Enclosure: ◄—— *Card*

NOTE: *You should prepare the buyer monthly costs estimate worksheet as a form to use during a buyer qualifying session.*
   This letter could be an e-mail or used as an attachment to an e-mail.

HOME BUYING SEMINAR—FREE

UR
H O M E   R E A L T Y

Home Buying Seminar

Many seminars charge hundreds of dollars to learn how to buy homes with low or even no down payment. [UR Home Realty] will show you how and a great deal more without cost or obligation.

Seminar includes the following:

- How to buy with no or low down payment.
- How large a loan can you obtain?
- What type of loan best meets your needs.
- What your total monthly housing costs will be.
- Obtaining a preapproval for a loan.
- [The difference between using a seller's agent or having your own agent in your search for your perfect home.]

[Thursday, October 4 at 7 P.M.]
[UR Home Realty]
[2734 East 24th Street]
[Eureka]

[Please RSVP (760) 300-8895. Seating is limited.]

NOTE: *This flyer can be distributed in rental areas and included as an enclosure to other letters.*

MARRIAGE OR ENGAGEMENT

UR
H O M E   R E A L T Y

_____   ←——— *Date and*
_____   *address*
_____
_____

Dear _____:

Congratulations on your recent [1. marriage 2. engagement]!

Need assistance in meeting any present or future housing needs? We have [rentals ranging from ($400) to ($4,000) a month and] homes that can be purchased with low and even no down payments and financing tailored to your particular needs.

I would like to offer you a housing consultation with no cost or obligation. This includes a needs analysis, market analysis, and prequalification for a housing loan if you decide to make a purchase. Please call me at [400-7610] if you would like to take advantage of this offer.

Yours truly,

_____

Enclosure: ◄——— *Card*

NEW PARENTS #1

UR
H O M E   R E A L T Y

_____
_____   ◄—— *Date and*
                         address
_____
_____

Dear _____ :

Congratulations on your new [1. son 2. daughter]!

Although I won't help out with the 2:00 A.M. feeding or the diapers, I can help you if you need more family space.

We have an unusually good selection of family homes, many of which allow flexible financing to meet individual buyers' needs. [Even "no down payment" is possible.]

Call me at [400-7610] to see how easy it can be to own your own single-family home with a [child-safe, fenced] backyard that is all yours.

Yours truly,

_____

Enclosure: ◄—— *Card*

NOTE: *Birth announcements in newspapers are particularly effective for targeting addresses of families who are living in apartments, condominiums, or mobile homes.*

NEW PARENTS #2

UR
H O M E   R E A L T Y

_____
_____ ←—— _Date and_
                          address
_____
_____

Dear _____:

Congratulations on the birth of your [1. son, (John) 2. daughter, (Mary-Jane)]!
It won't be long before [1. he 2. she] will be running around in seemingly
perpetual motion. Now is the time to consider a home with your own backyard for [1. John 2. Mary-Jane].

We presently have some great low- and even no-down payment opportunities. We can also help you prequalify for a home loan so that when you find
the property you want to call your home, you can be ready to act.

Are you interested? [1. I will be calling you in the next few days to discuss
your housing needs and provide financing information. 2. Call me today so I can
determine your housing needs and explain the various financing options presently available.]

Yours truly,

_____

Enclosure: ←—— _Card_

NOTE: _Birth announcements in newspapers are particularly effective for targeting_
addresses of families who are living in apartments, condominiums, or mobile homes.
_   Check the Do-Not-Call Registry before you indicate a call will be made._
Lower-income apartment dwellers are less likely to be on the registry than
higher-income homeowners.

OFFER TO AID IN TENANT RELOCATION

UR

H O M E   R E A L T Y

_____
_____   ← *Date and*
_____   *address*
_____

Dear _____:

I would like to offer my services to help you meet your relocation housing needs for rental or home purchase. [1. I will contact you in the next few days to tell you 2. Call me today if you want to learn] about low- and no-down payment home purchase opportunities, as well as what is available in the local rental market.

Yours truly,

_____

Enclosure: ◄── *Card*

NOTE: *This letter could be used when apartments are converted to cooperatives or condominiums, or when property is taken by eminent domain or razed for redevelopment. If the tenant is not on the Do-Not-Call Registry, use the phone for your contact.*

TENANT SOLICITATION—CONDOMINIUM CONVERSION

UR
H O M E   R E A L T Y

_____   ← *Date and*
_____   *address*

_____
_____

Dear _____:

Because [John Jones], the owner of your apartment building, [1. is in the process of converting your building to condominiums 2. has received approval to convert your building's units to cooperatives], you have a rare opportunity.

As the tenant you have the first opportunity to purchase your unit [with an exceptionally low down payment]. Besides being protected against future rent increases, you will be eligible for income tax deductions that will mean big savings to you. In addition, you, not the landlord will benefit by appreciation in value of your unit.

I will stop by to see you [this Saturday afternoon] to explain various financing options available and to show you how easy it will be to go from tenant to owner.

Yours truly,

_____

Enclosure: ← *Card*

NOTE: *The current tenants have three choices: (1) buy the unit they currently occupy; (2) buy somewhere else; or (3) find a new rental. Any of the available options presents an opportunity for an agent.*

LETTER TO NEIGHBOR AFTER RESIDENTIAL LISTING

UR
H O M E   R E A L T Y

_____
_____ ←— Date and
_____   address
_____

Dear _____ :

Our office has recently listed the home of your neighbor [John Jones] at [322 Maple Lane] for sale. You have probably noticed our For Sale sign.

I am writing you to ask for your help in locating a buyer for this fine home. In other words, you can help us find your new neighbor.

The home has [three bedrooms, two baths, and a den] [and, as you know, it has been lovingly cared for]. It is a great home that is priced right so anyone you suggest would be thankful for your recommendation. [1. I will be contacting you to see 2. Please contact me] if you can suggest any friends or acquaintances that might want to be your neighbor.

Thanking you in advance for your help,

_____

Enclosure: ←— Card

NOTE: Be certain to follow through by checking with the neighbors, if you indicate you will do so. If neighbors are not listed on the Do-Not-Call Registry, then your contact can be by phone. If listed, you will have to visit them.

LETTER TO FORMER RESIDENTIAL BUYER

UR
H O M E   R E A L T Y

_____ ← _Date and_
                    address
_____
_____
_____

Dear _____:

It is [almost one year] since you moved in to your new home in [Orchard Ridge]. [With what has happened to property values], I am certain you are pleased with your purchase.

The reason I am writing you is that a home in your neighborhood has just come on the market. It is a [3-year-old, 3BR, 2½ bath Spanish Ranch] at [9217 Westwood Place] priced at [$389,900].

I will be calling you in the next few days to see if you can suggest any friends or acquaintances that might want to be your new neighbors.

Your friendly real estate agent,

_____

Enclosure: ◄── _Card_

NOTE: _Even if the recipient is on the Do-Not-Call Registry, you can call within 18 months of a completed transaction._

OPEN HOUSE—INVITATION TO A NEIGHBOR

UR

H O M E   R E A L T Y

——————— ← *Date and*
——————— *address*
———————
———————

Dear ———————:

I would like you to [1. be my guest for coffee and cake   2. visit with me] on

[Sunday, October 12]

[1–4 P.M.]

at the [1. Johnson residence   2. former Johnson residence], [7413 Lynwood Avenue].

You will be able to view this fine home, which we are proud to offer for sale. Please bring any friends who might be interested in becoming your new neighbor. I look forward to seeing you!

Yours truly,

———————————

Enclosure: ◄— *Card*

NOTE: *A similar invitation can be sent to prospective buyers with whom you have had prior contact.*

OPEN HOUSE—VISITOR RATING FORM

Name: _____

Property: _____ Date: _____

Reason for visiting this open house ❑ advertising ❑ signs
  ❑ other (specify): _____

Features I particularly like: _____

_____

_____

Features I do not like: _____

_____

_____

Features I want that this property does not have: _____

_____

_____

I believe the price offering is: ❑ low ❑ about right ❑ high

Do you presently own your home? _____

Is it currently listed for sale with an agent? _____

General comments: _____

_____

_____

I would like to receive: ❑ e-mail ❑ phone calls on new listings before
  they are advertised to the general public.

Locations of interest: _____

_____

Special features desired: _____

Price range: _____ Phone number: _____
E-mail address: _____

NOTE: *This is a form rather than a letter. It is designed to obtain useful information for listing and selling. Of course, you should relay information concerning the property to the owner.*

By checking, the visitor is agreeing to contact by phone calls and/or e-mails on other properties. Many open-house viewers will be interested in receiving an e-mail of new listings before others know about them.

OPEN HOUSE—INVITATION TO PREVIOUS VISITOR

UR
H O M E   R E A L T Y

_____
_____   ← *Date and*
                 address
_____
_____

Dear _____ :

You visited one of our open houses on [October 7] at [37 Westwood Lane] in [Orchard Ridge].

I want to tell you about [1. several other 2. an] open house[s] we will have [this coming Saturday and Sunday], [October 14 and 15], from [11 A.M. to 4 P.M.].

[1. 7112 Hiawatha Drive]
[A 2,500+ Sq. Ft., 3-year-old Tuscany Mediterranean
with 3BR, den, and 2½ baths]
[$587,000]

[2. 3820 Thomas Circle]
[A 2,700 Sq. Ft., 1-year-new New England Colonial
with 4BR, 3 baths, and a 4-car garage]
[$612,000]

If you are interested in a new home, you will definitely want to see [1. this home 2. these two homes]. I think that you will be delighted with the area, the special features offered, and the value.

[Bring this letter with you and I will have (1. an LA Dodgers baseball cap 2. a special free gift) for you!]

Yours truly,

_____

Enclosure: ← *Card*

NOTE: *Letters such as this will increase open house traffic as well as show the owners that you are expending extra effort on their behalf. A free gift such as a baseball cap or a coffee mug with your firm's name on it will increase the effectiveness of the letter.*

If the open house visitor provided an e-mail address on the open house visitor rating (page 88) then e-mail notification would be appropriate. You could include a photo with the e-mail.

OPEN HOUSE—THANK YOU TO VISITOR

UR
H O M E   R E A L T Y

_____
_____   ◄— *Date and*
_____   *address*
_____

Dear _____:

I would like to thank you for visiting our firm's open house at [3714 Baxley Circle] [last weekend].

[I will be calling you to ask you your impression of the house and how it fits your needs.] I have enclosed information on several other available homes [as well as upcoming open houses]. If you are interested in any of them, I will be happy to arrange a showing.

Yours truly,

_____

Enclosures: ◄— *Card, property information*

NOTE: *A letter saying you will call forces a person to think about the call and what they will tell you. It is a power approach to letter writing. Do not call if the person is on the Do-Not-Call Registry and has not given permission to call (see permission authorization on Open House Visitor Rating Form on page 88).*

NOTICE OF SALE TO OPEN HOUSE VISITOR

UR
H O M E   R E A L T Y

←— *Date and address*

Dear _____ :

The open house you recently viewed at [69142 Sunrise Canyon Road] has just been sold. We have, however, recently received several very attractive new listings that I feel will be of great interest to you. I have enclosed information on several of these fine homes. You can view additional offerings [including virtual tours] by visiting our Web site [www.ur-home.net] [and clicking on the box "Homes for Sale"].

I feel certain I can find the perfect home for you as to size, location, price, and terms. [1. I will call you in the next few days to determine your specific housing needs so that I can begin to work for you. 2. Please call me so I can begin working to fulfill your housing needs.]

Yours truly,

_____

Enclosures: ◄— *Card, property information*

NOTE: *A letter saying you will call forces a person to think about the call and what they will tell you. It is a power approach to letter writing. Do not call if the person is on the Do-Not-Call Registry and has not given permission to call (see permission authorization on Open House Visitor Rating Form on page 88).*

CHAMBER OF COMMERCE INQUIRY

UR
H O M E   R E A L T Y

_____

◄——— *Date and*
            address

_____

_____

_____

Dear _____:

The [Midvale] Chamber of Commerce has indicated that you are considering becoming one of our neighbors.

Perhaps I am a bit premature, but I would like to welcome you to our community and offer you our relocation assistance. I would be happy to arrange motel reservations when you visit the area. If you desire any specific information, let me know.

Included is some general information about several of our housing opportunities. I have also enclosed a Housing Needs Checklist, which will help me in meeting your specific needs.

I suggest you check our Web site, [*www.ur-home.net*]. You can review the housing inventory presently available [and even take virtual tours through many of the properties].

Call me at [(800) 555-1111] for any additional information you would like.

Yours truly,

_____

Enclosures: ◄——— *Card, property information, Housing Needs Checklist*

NOTE: *See the Housing Needs Checklist on page 94. Having an office or personal 800 number greatly increases the likelihood of receiving a call. If the person is not listed on the Do-Not-Call Registry, a follow-up call should be made.*

HOUSING NEEDS CHECKLIST

UR
H O M E   R E A L T Y

Housing Needs Checklist

Presently I ❑ own a home ❑ rent

❑ I must sell before I relocate

❑ My home is currently listed for sale

I prefer to   ❑ rent   ❑ purchase

I prefer a(n)   ❑ single-family home   ❑ condominium   ❑ apartment

Estimated rental range: $ _____ to $ _____

Estimated purchase price:
    ❑ Under $150,000
    ❑ $150,000–$200,000
    ❑ $200,000–$300,000
    ❑ $300,000–$450,000
    ❑ $450,000–$700,000
    ❑ Over $700,000

Size of family: _____

Names and ages of children: _____ ; _____ ;
_____ ; _____ ; _____

Pets _____
Number of bedrooms desired: _____
Number of baths desired: _____
Particular locations I am interested in (if known): _____
_____

Required special features (disability, pets, hobbies, etc.): _____
_____

(1)

HOUSING NEEDS CHECKLIST *(continued)*

(2)

I expect to be

Checking the area around (date) _____

Relocating around (date) _____

❏ I would like to receive e-mails of new listings that appear to meet my requirements before the listings are advertised to the general public.

Name: _____

Address: _____

Phone: _____

NOTE: *This checklist can be used as an enclosure with the answer to any inquiry about property. The price range might need to be adjusted to reflect your local market.*

**OUT-OF-AREA BUYER INQUIRY—
BUYER AGENCY SOLICITATION**

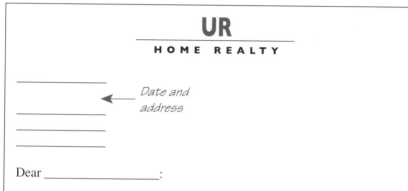

Dear _____:

I have [1. e-mailed 2. included] information you requested as to [present listings in (Westport Heights)].

Because agents whose duties are to get the best deal possible for the seller represent sellers, buyers need to have someone who will be primarily concerned with their interests.

I am a buyer's agent. I like to work with just a few buyers at a time devoting all of my efforts to meeting their needs.

While you might not have considered having your own agent, some of the advantages are as follows:

- I will help you separate and prioritize needs and wants.
- I will help you prequalify for a loan so that any offer you make will be from a position of strength.
- I will locate property available for purchase including property not available through seller's agents, which might include lender-owned property, property in foreclosure or probate, and even property for sale by owner.
- I will not waste your time viewing unsuitable property by showing you property to please an owner or because it is my own listing.
- I will analyze locations as to desirability considering your specific needs and interests.
- Prior to any offer, I will prepare a comparative market analysis to determine fair value range of the property. A price asked by a seller might bear little relationship to actual value.

(1)

OUT-OF-AREA BUYER INQUIRY—
BUYER AGENCY SOLICITATION (continued)

(2)

- Before you sign anything, I will make certain you fully understand your financial obligations.

- I will make purchase recommendations as to property as well as the price to be offered with the goal of obtaining the property that suits you best at the lowest price; of course, all decisions will be yours.

- I will use my experience to protect you against unfair contracts including seller fraud.

- I will advise you throughout the negotiating process.

- I will make certain the property is as represented by recommending an inspection by a qualified home inspector.

- I will explain various financing options and types of loans available and will recommend loan types and lenders based solely on your best interests and not on any personal interest on my part.

- I will help and advise you throughout the financing process.

- I will monitor the closing process to make certain everything is accomplished as agreed.

What Does Agency Cost You?

In most cases, nothing. When the seller has listed with an agent, which is the case in most sales, my fee is paid out of the seller's pocket, not yours.

I have enclosed an agency agreement. By signing and returning [three] copies, you can have your own agent working for you.

I will be calling you to answer any questions you may have. To find out more about [UR Home Realty] and me, visit our Web site at [www.ur-home.net].

Yours truly,

_____

Enclosures: ◄— Card, agency agreement

NOTE: While the letter is long, a list format will encourage the recipient to read it in full.

BUYER AGENCY FLYER

How Can Buyers Protect Themselves?

Did you know that the real estate agent who advertises a property, shows the property to a buyer, helps the buyer make decisions, and prepares the purchase offer doesn't necessarily have the buyer's best interests in mind? That's right, the helpful agent could be the exclusive agent of the seller with agency duties to get the best deal possible for the seller with no agency duties whatsoever to the buyer.

As a buyer, you can protect yourself by having a buyer's agent where your interests, not the seller's interests, are of paramount importance.

Having your own agent has the following advantages:

- Your time is not wasted by an agent showing you unsuitable property to impress owners with the agent's activity or who wants to push his or her own listings, which will mean more dollars for the agent rather than working for what is best for you.

- Your agent will work with you so you are prequalified for a loan and know purchase limits.

- You are not going to be limited to properties listed for sale by agents. You will be exposed to properties that may be in probate or foreclosure, properties owned by lenders, and even properties for sale by owners.

- Your agent will analyze properties based on your needs and provide value estimates based on the market.

- Your agent will recommend properties to be considered and what should be offered and prepare the offer with your interests in mind.

- Your own agent will make certain you fully understand all aspects of a purchase contract before it is signed.

- Negative aspects of a property will be evaluated, and your agent will make certain that your offer is subject to a professional property inspection.

(1)

BUYER AGENCY FLYER *(continued)*

(2)

- Your agent will recommend the type of loan that best meets your needs and will work with you in locating the most advantageous loan terms.

- Your agent will be in contact with the lender, the seller, and the closing agent to avoid any problems during the closing process.

What Does It Cost to Have Your Own Agent?

In most cases the fee paid your agent will be totally paid by the seller rather than taken from your pocket.

We are proud to be buyer's agents. To find out more about us and buyer representation, check our Web site, [*www.ur-home.net*].

[UR Home Realty]
[1102 Bigelow Street]
[800-555-2646]
[*name@ur-home.net*]

NOTE: *This flyer can be given to persons inquiring about properties and be used as a mailing attachment.*

CHAPTER

LAND, BUSINESS, AND INVESTMENT BUYER SOLICITATION

BUILDER SOLICITATION—LOTS

UR
H O M E   R E A L T Y

_____
                    ◄─── *Date and*
_____   *address*
_____
_____

Dear _____:

We have recently listed [20] lots in [Midvale Heights]. The lots all have [sewer and water installed and paid for], and they are competitively priced from [$67,500 to $92,500, with interesting terms possible].

I will be calling you in the next few days to discuss a convenient time to show you these desirable building sites.

Yours truly,

_____

Enclosure: ◄─── *Card*

NOTE: *The letter takes for granted the reader's interest, and the mention of a phone call forces the reader to spend a few seconds on the idea of lots in the area specified. The phone call should offer the choice of time of showing, not ask whether the builder wants a showing.*

The Do-Not-Call Registry applies only to residential calls and not to business calls made to non-residential numbers.

ADJOINING OWNER SOLICITATION

UR
H O M E   R E A L T Y

_____   ← *Date and*
_____   *address*
_____
_____

Dear _____:

I have just listed the property at [111 Midvale Lane] for sale. Because this property adjoins your property, we felt that you should have the first opportunity to purchase it. I am therefore notifying you before we advertise to the general public.

I am certain that you understand the advantage of owning this adjoining parcel. I will contact you in the next few days to provide you with any specific information you might desire.

Yours truly,

_____

Enclosure: ◄—— *Card*

NOTE: *This letter is a teaser. It creates urgency and a desire to know the price. This approach can be used for raw land, lots, farms, and even income or investment property. A great many properties are sold to adjoining property owners.*

OWNER OF SIMILAR INVESTMENT PROPERTY IN AREA

_____
UR
H O M E   R E A L T Y

_____
_____   ◄——— *Date and*
                                     address
_____
_____

Dear _____ :

When we listed the [24-unit apartment building at 3305–3307 Chestnut Boulevard], I immediately thought that this would be the ideal investment for the owner of the property at [3309 Chestnut Boulevard].

Because the property is [1. right next door to your property 2. so close to your property and is so similar], the management advantages of dual ownership are apparent.

The property is available at [1. an attractive price with flexible terms 2. $1.5 million with approximately ($150,000) down 3. a price and terms that will allow an immediate positive cash flow]. I will be contacting you in the next few days to discuss the advantages that this fine property can offer you.

Yours truly,

_____

P.S. If you are not interested in purchasing this property, perhaps you would consider selling your property. The advantages to a buyer owning both investment properties could make for an exceptional sale opportunity.

Enclosure: ◄——— *Card*

NOTE: *The P.S. raises the point that if the readers aren't buyers, they should be sellers. It also reinforces the advantages of owning two similar properties.*

COMMERCIAL TENANT SOLICITATION OF OWNERSHIP

UR
H O M E   R E A L T Y

_____
         ⟵ *Date and*
_____   *address*

_____

_____

Dear [Ms. Perkins]:

How would you like your office to be in [1. Perkins Plaza 2. the Perkins Building] and not have to move?

Your present [1. office 2. commercial] building has just been placed on the market. It offers you a rare opportunity. You can be your own landlord and be entitled to depreciation, income, and appreciation instead of just a growing pile of rent receipts.

I will contact you in the next few days to show you how [Perkins Plaza] can become a reality.

Yours truly,

_____

Enclosures:　　⟵ *Card, photo*

NOTE: *This letter should be sent to professional tenants and strong retail tenants. It has an excellent approach to pride by naming the building after the solicited buyer. Utilize your computer to put the tenant's name and/or logo on a digital photo of the building.*

TENANT SOLICITATION—OFFICE CONDOMINIUM

UR
H O M E   R E A L T Y

_____   ⟵ _Date and_
_____   _address_
_____
_____

Dear _____:

Do you realize that you could move your office [less than three blocks] away and have the following:

- Absolute protection against future rent increases
- The tax advantage of depreciation
- Payments that increase your equity rather than worthless rent receipts
- An investment that will likely show exceptional appreciation
- A hedge against inflation

I have [1. several 2. an] outstanding office condominium[s] for sale that offer[s] you advantages that a rental cannot provide, and [1. is 2. are] bound to please your accountant. I should be able to make you an owner with little or no increase in actual monthly costs and a down payment tailored to your needs.

This may sound too good to be true, but I will prove it to you and your accountant. You can avoid saying "I should have . . . " in the future by investigating now.

I will be calling you to give you more information on this very special opportunity.

Yours truly,

_____

Enclosure: ⟵ _Card_

NOTE: _By canvassing the buildings close to your listing or by using a reverse directory, you can put together a sizable mailing list._
The Do-Not-Call Registry does not apply to nonresidential phone calls.

FRANCHISE—GENERAL NEEDS

To:	
From:	agent@urhomerealty.net
Subject:	Your Real Estate Needs

Attention: Real Estate Officer

I would like to be your real estate eyes and ears in [the Clark and Humboldt Counties].

If you would let me know your real estate needs regarding size, traffic count, access, demographics, price, rent, and so on, I would be happy to put my area knowledge to work for you.

Yours truly,

_____

NOTE: *Names and addresses of franchises are readily available from the Internet. One site to consider for names and addresses is* www.bison1.com/franchisepass.html. *An e-mail approach should be considered.*

FRANCHISE—SPECIFIC LOCATION

To:	
From:	agent@urhomerealty.net
Subject:	Excellent Franchise Location

Dear _____:

Our office has recently listed [a property at (55 Chestnut Boulevard)]. Click here for specific property information. Because of [access and traffic], I feel that it would be an excellent location for one of your franchises. An attractive [1. purchase price 2. lease] is available. Please let me know if you are interested.

I am willing to work with you in meeting your real estate needs within [Dade County]. If you could let me know your specific interests, my eyes, ears, and expertise are available for you.

Yours truly,

_____

NOTE: *See note on previous letter.*

WHITE ELEPHANT INVESTMENT

UR
H O M E   R E A L T Y

_____   ← *Date and*
_____   *address*
_____
_____

Dear _____ :

Do you know

What to Do with a White Elephant?

We are looking for an investor with vision who can create a productive use for [a seven-story, 74,000-square-foot former textile plant with rail siding on a six-acre site north of Highway 30].

Although it's a problem, the price of [$890,000] reflects that. If you have a solution, someone else's problem can be your opportunity.

I will contact you in the next few days to arrange a private showing and perhaps we can brainstorm a solution to the problem.

Yours truly,

_____

Enclosure: ◄— *Card*

NOTE: *This is an excellent letter for owners of property in the area, creative investors, and developers. A letter such as this intrigues investors and speculators. It presents a puzzle to be solved. It is an excellent way to gain initial personal access to major buyers of investment property.*

SAFE INVESTMENT—NET LEASE

UR
H O M E   R E A L T Y

_____   ← _Date and_
_____   _address_
_____
_____

Dear _____:

Do you want

Monotonous Income?

Would you like rent checks, month after month, year after year while the tenant pays the taxes and makes the repairs? Would you like an investment where there are no decisions for you to make?

Would you like to take full advantage of the tax code and shelter spendable dollars from taxation and/or pay taxes on your gains at a sharply reduced rate?

If a hands-off, tax friendly investment guaranteed by a financially strong tenant interests you and you can handle a [$250,000] down payment, then this could be the investment you have been waiting for.

I will be contacting you in the next few days, if you don't call me first, to arrange a private showing of a very special opportunity.

Yours truly,

_____

Enclosure: ◄— _Card_

NOTE: _As written, this solicitation is for a triple-net property leased to a strong tenant._

Mailings should be to investors owning larger quality properties as well as high-income individuals such as doctors, attorneys, and CPAs. A letter such as this allows you to expand the size and quality of your list of potential real estate investors. Call recipients at their business rather than their residence to avoid Do-Not-Call Registry restrictions.

$1,000,000 INVESTMENT

UR

H O M E   R E A L T Y

_____

_____ ◄— *Date and*
                     address
_____

_____

Dear _____:

Want something

Better than a Money Market Account?

If a [million-dollar] price doesn't frighten you, I have a real estate investment that offers the following:

- [A financially strong tenant]
- A hedge against inflation
- Great leverage opportunities
- Tax-sheltered income
- Likely appreciation
- [Professional management]

I will call you within the next few days to discuss the benefits offered by this extraordinary real estate investment.

Yours truly,

_____

Enclosure: ◄— *Card*

NOTE: *Income will be sheltered by depreciation. The Do-Not-Call Registry regulations apply to residential calls but not to business phones.*

REFERRAL INVESTOR

UR
H O M E   R E A L T Y

_____ ← *Date and*
_____   *address*
_____
_____

Dear _____ :

[Alice Smith] recommended that I contact you. We have [1. just listed
2. available] an exceptional investment opportunity that [she] thought might
interest you.

It is a [low-risk] property offering the [possibility of extraordinary appreciation
coupled with tax-sheltered income]. It would require a down payment of
around [$110,000].

[1. I will be contacting you 2. Call me today if you would like] to determine if
this property would fulfill your investment needs.

Yours truly,

_____

Enclosure: ◄—— *Card*

NOTE: *This letter gives little detail other than amount of down payment. It is
intended to get the recipients to consider owning investment property and to
prepare them so you can qualify them according to their specific needs. Although
you must have an actual property, the letter is used to tantalize. Providing more
details would increase the likelihood that the recipient will interpret some of
those details as negative.*

Again, be aware of the Do-Not-Call Registry regulations.

SYNDICATE FORMATION

_____

UR
H O M E   R E A L T Y

_____

_____ ← *Date and*
_____ *address*
_____
_____

Dear _____ :

I am putting together a small group of local investors [1. to take part in an exceptional investment opportunity as limited partners 2. to take advantage of the exceptional opportunities available now in distressed income property]. [1. (Joe Jones) has recommended you as a person who would appreciate taking part in this opportunity. 2. You indicated some time ago that I should contact you if a really great opportunity presented itself.]

Because you are knowledgeable in investment matters, you will understand the desirability of a prime [low-risk] real estate investment [at a bargain basement price].

Investors must be able to make a [$100,000] minimum investment. [1. I will call you to determine your interest in 2. Please call me at (400-7610) if you are interested in] attending an informal meeting of potential investors at my home at [1744 Midvale Lane] on [Saturday morning, April 10 at 10 A.M.]. After I have discussed the opportunity and answered any questions, those who are interested will have an opportunity to visit the property.

Yours truly,

_____

Enclosure: ← *Card*

NOTE: *A morning home meeting provides a nonthreatening atmosphere. Also, forming a group meeting tends to reduce apprehension. For a syndicate solicitation, be certain that you have checked your state laws. Syndicates may be subject to federal and state registration unless they fit into an exemption. Consult an attorney before you attempt to form a syndicate. Calls should be to business phones or the Do-Not-Call Registry will have to be consulted.*

NOTICE TO BUSINESS OWNER OF
RELATED BUSINESS FOR SALE

UR
H O M E   R E A L T Y

_____ ← _Date and_
_____   _address_
_____
_____

Dear _____:

Because you are in the [retail hardware] business, you now have an exceptional opportunity for expansion.

We have just listed for sale a [successful hardware store] that offers great potential. The books are open to you and your accountant. I will be calling you with more details. I believe that this opportunity deserves your immediate attention.

Yours truly,

_____

Enclosure: ◄— _Card_

NOTE: _This letter is a teaser to excite interest. The letter should give very little information about the business, and the letter should not identify the particular business being offered at this time._

Keep in mind that financial information concerning a property or business should never be given out to anyone without the owner's permission.

SUPPLIER OR WHOLESALER—BUSINESS OPPORTUNITY

UR

H O M E   R E A L T Y

←   Date and
address

Dear _____ :

Because you are a [plumbing] [1. distributor 2. wholesaler], I thought that you should be aware of the [plumbing supply business] we recently listed for sale. [Jones Plumbing Supplies] is located at [105 Midvale], and the price of [$250,000] includes [all fixtures, vehicles, and an advantageous lease]. The books are open to a qualified buyer [and owner financing is possible].

I will call you in the next few days to ask for your help in identifying any of your customers who might be interested in an exceptional expansion opportunity.

Yours truly,

_____

Enclosure: ◄— _Card_

NOTE: _Suppliers have a stake in finding a buyer because a happy buyer will feel indebted to the supplier. Many businesses are sold to buyers based on information gained from suppliers._

For a supplier letter, the business should be identified, and a price or price range should be indicated.

OPERATING INCOME AND EXPENSES

UR
H O M E   R E A L T Y

FAX

To: _____

From: _____

Date: _____

Attn: _____

Pages w/cover: _____

Dear _____:

The following is a statement of income and expenses for the property located at [19 Partridge Lane] [in accord with your request]. The figures set forth are based on [1. a copy of the latest tax return provided by the owner 2. a statement provided by the owner 3. the books provided to us by the owner 4. the property management statements 5. information furnished by the owner's accountant].

Income

Scheduled gross annual income	$ _____
Vacancy and collection loss	($ _____)
Adjusted gross annual income	$ _____

Expenses

Taxes [2004]	$ _____
Insurance cost [2004]	$ _____
Policy provider [Jones Underwriters]	
Utilities [2004]	$ _____
Management costs [2004]	$ _____
Maintenance and repairs [2004]	$ _____
Total expenses	($ _____)
[(before debt service)]	
Net operating income	$ _____
[(not considering debt service)]	

(1)

OPERATING INCOME AND EXPENSES *(continued)*

(2)

It should be pointed out that just a [3] percent annual increase in rents would increase the net income by [over $50,000] within [six] years, and rentals in the area have been experiencing an annual increase of [over three] percent a year.

I will be calling you to answer any questions you may have and to show you why I feel this investment opportunity deserves your immediate and serious consideration.

Yours truly,

_____

Enclosure: ◄—— *Card*

NOTE: *Minor modification would turn this letter into an operating income and expense statement to be attached to property briefs (flyers describing properties).*
   This information could be provided by e-mail or fax.
   Of course, you must have an owner's permission to give out income and expense data.

SERVICING THE LISTING

Time is generally not a critical factor in letters to owners regarding servicing the listing unless they deal with a purchase offer. Letters provide a hard copy record of your owner contacts. Should time be important, then the phone, e-mail, or fax should be used for communication.

THANK YOU FOR LISTING

UR
H O M E R E A L T Y

Date and address ←

Dear _____:

As the broker with [UR Home Realty], I appreciate the confidence you have shown by making [UR Home Realty] your exclusive agent for the sale of your home.

I want you to know you can expect us to be diligent and professional in our efforts to make a favorable sale on your [home]. We have already [1. prepared initial advertising 2. placed initial advertising 3. included a virtual tour of your home on our Web site (_www.ur-home.net_)] and provided information on your home to [our multiple-listing service]. We will keep you up-to-date on our progress.

[Mr. Lynn Smith] of our office will be working with you throughout the sales process and even after the sale to ensure a satisfactory closing. If you have any questions concerning your property or our efforts, please contact [Mr. Smith].

I look forward to presenting you with a buyer.

Yours truly,

_____

Enclosure: ← _Card_

THANK YOU FOR LISTING—OUT-OF-TOWN OWNER

UR
H O M E   R E A L T Y

_____   *Date and*
             ◄——   *address*
_____

_____

_____

Dear _____:

I would like to thank you for showing your confidence in [UR Home Realty] by appointing us your exclusive agent for the sale of your property. We have already entered your [home] on [*www.ur-home.net*]. Information about your home is now available to millions of home hunters on a global basis. Locally, the [Westhaven Board of REALTORS®] has [712] agents in [57] offices who want to sell your home.

Because you live a great distance from our office, would you please provide us with the following information?

1. The name and phone number of a local person to contact in the event of an emergency _____

2. The name and address of your property insurance agent and policy number _____

3. The name and phone number of your local attorney (*if applicable*) _____

4. The name and phone number for applicable
   - gardening services _____
   - pool service _____
   - protection service _____
   - pest control service _____
   - cleaning and maintenance service _____
   - homeowner association _____

(1)

THANK YOU FOR LISTING—OUT-OF-TOWN OWNER *(continued)*

(2)

5. Your fax number _____

   If you don't have a fax, give the name and fax number of an office service center, such as Kinko's, where a fax can be sent to you.

   Name: _____   Fax: _____

6. Your cell phone number _____

7. Your e-mail address _____

You should contact your insurance agent to make certain that you are maintaining adequate coverage.

I look forward to telling you that your [home] has been sold.

Sincerely,

_____

Enclosure: ◄——— *Card*

NEIGHBORHOOD INFORMATION REQUEST

UR
H O M E   R E A L T Y

_____ ← *Date and*
_____ *address*
_____
_____

Dear _____:

Having an in-depth knowledge of your neighborhood and neighbors can give us a competitive edge over less informed sales agents who represent other properties.

We value your knowledge of your community and would therefore appreciate if you would share this knowledge by completing this form to the best of your ability to help us sell your home.

1. Neighborhood features you feel a buyer would be most pleased with:
   _____
   _____

2. School districts: _____

3. School bus stops: _____

4. Names, ages, and schools attended by neighborhood children (include private schools):
   _____   _____   _____
   _____   _____   _____
   _____   _____   _____
   _____   _____   _____
   _____   _____   _____

5. Youth activities in the area (Little League, junior hockey, soccer league, etc.): _____

6. Public recreational facilities in the area (parks, pools, playgrounds, tennis courts, etc.): _____

(1)

NEIGHBORHOOD INFORMATION REQUEST *(continued)*

(2)

7. Nearest public transportation route: _____

8. Nearest medical facility: _____

9. Nearest community center (for children, seniors, etc.): _____
   _____

10. Nearest houses of worship: _____

11. Nearest shopping area: _____

12. General information on closest neighbors: _____
    _____

13. The professions of people living in area that might interest a possible buyer (doctor, banker, attorney, professor, or another professional):
    _____

14. Describe the interests of the person or family you feel would best appreciate your home and neighborhood: _____
    _____

15. Other information that would be of interest to a likely buyer:
    _____
    _____

Please send your completed form to my attention in the enclosed postage-paid envelope.

We greatly appreciate your help in providing this information about your neighborhood.

Appreciatively yours,

_____

Enclosure: ◄—— *Card*

NOTE: *Not only does this letter gain you sales ammunition, it also shows the owner that you appreciate the neighborhood and neighbors and are making your best efforts on their behalf.*

INSTRUCTION SHEET TRANSMITTAL

UR
H O M E   R E A L T Y

_____
_____   ←— *Date and*
_____   *address*
_____

Dear _____:

In marketing your home, we are competing against [1. dozens 2. hundreds] of other owners who are all after the same pool of buyers. To compete successfully, we want to gain every possible advantage. The enclosed instruction sheet allows you to play an important role in obtaining the best possible sale for your home.

Please call me if you have any questions.

Thanking you in advance for your cooperation,

_____

Enclosures: ←— *Card, homeowner instructions*

HOMEOWNER INSTRUCTIONS

UR
HOME REALTY

Homeowner Hints for a Successful Sale

I. Exterior

   A. Grass and shrubs. Keep trimmed. Consider a fast-greening fertilizer such as ammonium sulfate (inexpensive) for a deep green lawn.

   B. Pets. If you have a dog, clean up any dog dirt on a daily basis. If you have a cat, change the litter box daily. Pets should be restrained or kept away from the property when it is to be shown.

   C. Fences. Make any needed repairs. A neat, well-painted fence gives a positive impression.

   D. Flowers. Plant seasonal blooming flowers, especially near the front door and in any patio area. A profusion of color can have your home half-sold before the door is even opened.

   E. Bird feeders. Hummingbird feeders and bird houses create a pleasant mood, especially when they are close to any patio area.

   F. Paint. Concentrating on the following two areas may be the most profitable:

      1. Front door. Front door should be refinished or painted if it shows excessive wear.

      2. Condition of exterior paint. Often only the trim or, depending on sun exposure, only one or two sides of the house need painting. Keep in mind that paint is cheap compared to the extra dollars a home with a clean, fresh appearance will bring.

   G. Lawn furniture. Place lawn furniture and barbeque in an attractive, leisurely manner. A badminton net or croquet set-up gives a positive image as well.

   H. Roof. If the roof needs to be repaired or replaced, it's best to have the work done. Otherwise, buyers will want to deduct the cost even if your price already reflects the required work. Delaying repairs can actually cost you twice as much.

(1)

HOMEOWNER INSTRUCTIONS *(continued)*

(2)

II. Interior

A. Housekeeping. Because you are competing against model homes, your home must look as much like a model as possible. Floors, bath fixtures, and appliances must be sparkling. Consider using a car wax on appliances. Make beds early in the day. Unmade beds and late sleepers create a very negative image.

B. Odors and aromas. Avoid heavy frying, using vinegar, or cooking strong-smelling foods. Odors often last and work against the image you are trying to create. On the other hand, some smells have a positive effect on people: Baked bread, apple pie, chocolate cookies, and cinnamon rolls are examples of foods that can help sell your home. Consider keeping packaged cookie or bread dough in the refrigerator. Just before a scheduled showing, the smell of these baking foods can be a great help to us. If you or your family members smoke, don't smoke in your home and don't allow guests to smoke. Stale tobacco odors can be masked with some odor sprays. If the temperature allows it, open windows and air out the house every morning.

C. Paint. If you have leftover paint, you can accomplish a great deal by doing touch-ups where needed. If the surface is dark, repaint with light colors such as off-white, oyster, light beige, or pale yellow. Light colors make rooms appear fresh as well as larger.

D. Plumbing. Repair any leaky faucets. Make certain that you don't have a gurgling toilet.

E. Shades and blinds. Replace any torn shades or broken blinds.

F. Drapes. If drapes need cleaning, have it done. If they are old and worn, stained or dark, consider replacing them with either light-colored drapes or off-white vinyl vertical blinds. (Large discount and home improvement centers usually carry standard sizes at reasonable prices.)

G. Carpets. Dirty carpets should be either professionally steam-cleaned (preferred), or you should rent a heavy-duty cleaner. If the carpet is badly worn, replace it with new carpet (and a quality pad) in a neutral color. Consider either a plush or Berber carpet.

H. Lighting. If any room appears dark, increase the wattage of your light bulbs. Before a showing, open the blinds and drapes and turn on the lights, even during the day—you want the house as bright as possible. Be sure that your light fixtures and windows are clean.

HOMEOWNER INSTRUCTIONS *(continued)*

(3)

I. **Closets.** If closets appear crowded, remove items not needed and put in boxes. They can be stacked neatly in a corner of the basement, attic, or garage.

J. **Too much furniture.** Many homes appear crowded, with too many pieces of large furniture and too much bric-a-brac. Consider putting excess furniture in a storage locker.

K. **Garage and basement.** Spruce up your work area. Consider a garage sale to get rid of items you no longer need. Put excess items in boxes and stack them neatly in a corner. Consider using a commercial garage floor cleaner on oil and grease marks on the garage floor and driveway. You might consider a commercial steam cleaner (not a carpet cleaner).

L. **Temperature.** On cold days, a natural fire in the fireplace will help us sell your home. Start the fire before the showing is scheduled.
On hot days, consider turning the air conditioner four to five degrees cooler than normal. The contrast will seem phenomenal, making a very positive impression. In moderate weather, open windows for fresh air.

III. Your Best Role During Showings

A. When your home is shown, it's best that you disappear. Buyers feel restrained with an owner present. If buyers hesitate to voice their concerns, then their questions cannot be answered and their problems cannot be solved.

B. If you must remain, try to stay in one area. Excellent places to be are working in the garden, on the lawn, or in the workshop. These activities create a positive image. While soft music is fine, turn off the TV.

C. *Never, never* follow the agent around the house during the showing, volunteer any information, or answer questions the buyers ask the agent. You have engaged professional real estate salespeople. We will ask you questions if necessary.

[UR Home Realty]
[555-8200]

NOTE: *Besides using these instructions as an enclosure with a letter, you can also use them as part of your listing presentation or as a handout after listing.*

MARKETING PLAN FOR HOME

UR
H O M E   R E A L T Y

⟵ *Date and address*

Dear _____:

I would like to share with you our marketing plan for your home.

- Install sign [and talking sign].

- Take photographs of your home.

- Give you suggestions to help increase the marketability of your home.

- Prepare a property brief (descriptive sheet) with a photo of your home emphasizing the desirable characteristics of the property.

- Place [1. photo 2. virtual tour] of your home, along with detailed information, on our office Web site [www.ur-home.net] as well as at least [three] other Web sites covering local, regional, and national properties.

- Install a lockbox on the property to aid in showing your home to prospective buyers when you are not available.

- Send property briefs to other agents active in the area and discuss with them the benefits your home has to offer.

- Leave a supply of property briefs at your home for open house visitors and agent showings.

- Prepare a minimum of three separate classified ads for your home.

- Schedule ad placement.

- Meet with you to show you how you can help in the marketing of your home.

- Prepare for and conduct [our office agent visitation and] board visitation by real estate agents.

(1)

MARKETING PLAN FOR HOME *(continued)*

(2)

- Discuss your home with agents who toured your home to find ways to enhance its marketability.

- Our agents will call or e-mail all likely prospects they are currently working with about your home.

- Send direct mailings to area neighbors to enlist help in selecting a new neighbor.

- Prepare for and conduct an open house.

- Follow up on all leads generated by calls about or visits to your home.

- Make weekly calls to all agents who used the lockbox about the interest of their buyers.

- Communicate [weekly] with you on our efforts and progress with your home as well as changes in the area market.

- Advertise your home along with other homes in your area and in the same price range, as well as continue our program of institutional advertising.

- Continue to make our best efforts to locate a buyer as well as internally evaluate those efforts until we are successful.

If you have any questions about this marketing plan outline, please call me.

Yours truly,

_____

Enclosure: ◄—— *Card*

NOTE: *You could use this as an attachment to a letter to an owner thanking him or her for the listing as well as a tool to obtain listings.*

SELLER'S NET PROCEEDS ESTIMATE TRANSMITTAL

UR
H O M E   R E A L T Y

_____   ← *Date and*
_____   *address*
_____
_____

Dear _____:

Enclosed is a seller's net proceeds worksheet I have prepared for your property at [41 Greer Street].

The net reflects [your present mortgage being paid off and a sale at the list price of ($239,000)].

I believe the figures on the worksheet are reliable, but they are estimates only and are not guaranteed.

If you have any questions, please call me.

Yours truly,

_____

Enclosures: ◄— *Card, Seller Net Proceeds Estimate Worksheet*

NOTE: *Ordinarily the seller's net information should be given to the owner at the time the listing is taken.*

SELLER'S NET PROCEEDS ESTIMATE WORKSHEET

Estimated Seller's Net

Credits		Debits	
Sale price	$_____	Loans	$_____
Impound account balance	$_____	Other encumbrances	$_____
		Loan prepayment	$_____
Prepaid insurance	$_____	penalties	
Prepaid taxes	$_____	Agent fees	$_____
Other credits	$_____	Escrow/attorney	$_____
Total credits	$_____	Abstract/title insurance	$_____
		Transfer tax	$_____
		Termite inspection	$_____
		Real estate taxes	$_____
		Unpaid assessments	$_____
		Home protection plan	$_____
		Other	$_____
		Total debits	$_____
		Total credits	$_____
		Total debits	$_____
		Seller net	$_____

NOTE: *Seller net would be cash and/or carryback financing in which the seller is financing the buyer.*

AGENT PROPERTY EVALUATION TRANSMITTAL LETTER

UR

H O M E   R E A L T Y

_____   ◄─── *Date and*
_____   *address*
_____
_____

Dear _____:

Enclosed are copies of agent property evaluations made by agents at our
[1. office caravan (and the) 2. multiple-listing service caravan] on [October 14].
The evaluations can provide valuable information about your home.

I will be contacting you in the next few days to discuss these evaluations.

Yours truly,

_____

Enclosures: ◄─── *Card, agent property evaluations*

AGENT PROPERTY EVALUATION

Property Address: _____   Date: _____

Name of Owner(s): _____

   1. Feature of the home that will be most appealing to buyer:

      _____

      _____

      _____

      _____

   2. Features or lack of features that buyers are likely to view as a negative:

      _____

      _____

      _____

      _____

   3. I feel that the price is ❏ too high ❏ too low ❏ realistic

      By how much? $ _____   Why? _____

      _____

      _____

   4. To increase salability, the owner should consider:

      _____

      _____

      _____

      _____

NOTE: *Give this form to agents who view the home at office or MLS caravans as well as those who attend an agent open house. You would fill in the property address and name of owner. Give the completed form to the owner.*

WEB SITE INFORMATION TRANSMITTAL

UR

H O M E   R E A L T Y

_____

<------- *Date and*
              address

_____

_____

_____

Dear _____:

Enclosed is a printout of the information about your home that we have posted on our Web site, [*www.ur-home.net*]. Features of the Web site include the ability [1. to view several photos of your home 2. to enlarge photos 3. for a viewer to have a virtual tour of your home moving from room to room as in a physical viewing].

We have also posted the Web site material to the additional Web sites [*www.PalmSpringsHomes.com, www.CARealtor.com, www.SuCasa.net, and www.Realtor.com*].

As the world becomes technology-oriented, the Internet has increased in value as a marketing tool. However, this is just one of many marketing tools we will employ to sell your home. You will see other methods in your [weekly] progress reports.

Looking forward to a successful sale,

_____

Enclosures: <------- *Card, Web site printout of owner's home*

AD COPY TRANSMITTAL

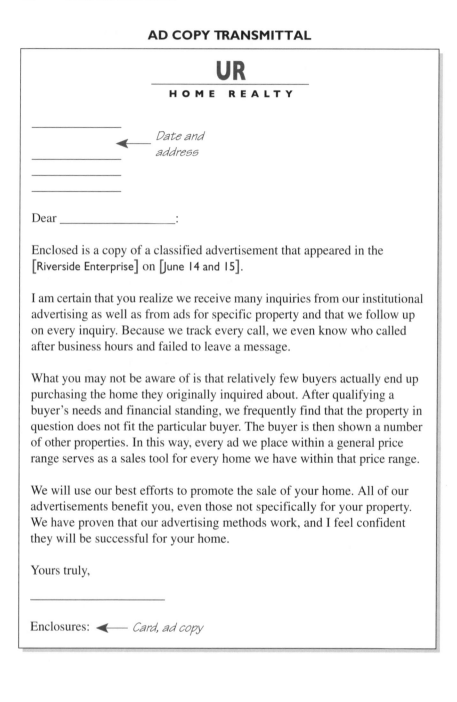

UR
H O M E   R E A L T Y

_____   ← _Date and_
_____   _address_
_____
_____

Dear _____:

Enclosed is a copy of a classified advertisement that appeared in the [Riverside Enterprise] on [June 14 and 15].

I am certain that you realize we receive many inquiries from our institutional advertising as well as from ads for specific property and that we follow up on every inquiry. Because we track every call, we even know who called after business hours and failed to leave a message.

What you may not be aware of is that relatively few buyers actually end up purchasing the home they originally inquired about. After qualifying a buyer's needs and financial standing, we frequently find that the property in question does not fit the particular buyer. The buyer is then shown a number of other properties. In this way, every ad we place within a general price range serves as a sales tool for every home we have within that price range.

We will use our best efforts to promote the sale of your home. All of our advertisements benefit you, even those not specifically for your property. We have proven that our advertising methods work, and I feel confident they will be successful for your home.

Yours truly,

_____

Enclosures: ←— _Card, ad copy_

PROGRESS REPORT

UR
H O M E   R E A L T Y

_____
_____ ← Date and
_____   address
_____
_____

Dear _____ :

This note is to keep you informed of our efforts on your behalf. During the [week] of [September 4–10], we have

1. advertised your home in [two newspapers] using [three] ads with insertions on [11] days. [This is in addition to our institutional advertising and ads for other property in the same price range.]

2. answered [51] inquiries on your home and have had [seven] showings by our own salespeople.

3. had [five] showings by salespeople from cooperating offices.

4. had [one] open house and registered [17] guests.

5. kept your home active in the Midvale Multiple-Listing Service Web site available to [107] offices and more than [1,000] salespeople, as well as on [three] Web sites covering regional and national properties, plus our own site [www.ur-home.net].

6. followed up on every lead received from a variety of sources.

[Although we have not yet received an offer on your home,] we are very optimistic and will continue our efforts on your behalf.

Yours truly,

_____

Enclosure: ◄— Card

WEEKLY PROGRESS REPORT (FORM)

UR
H O M E   R E A L T Y

⟵ *Date and address*

Dear _____:

The following weekly progress report describes our marketing efforts for your [home].

[Week ending]: [7 August]
Property: [3961 Hampton Lane]
Owners: [Mr. and Mrs. J.C. Clark]
Number of phone inquiries: [13]
Number of showings by our office: [3]
Advertising: [2 ads in Daily Sentinel as well as feature in Home Showcase and 4 Web sites]
Electronic lockbox activity: [5 showings by other offices]

Open House
Date(s): [5 August]
Number of visitors: [8]
Comments of other agents and prospective buyers: [Great neighborhood and lovely patio. Carpeting will have to be replaced by buyer and kitchen could use new countertop. One prospect indicated wallpaper was dated and should be removed.]

If you have any questions, please contact me.

Yours truly,

_____

Enclosure: ⟵ *Card*

NOTE: *Some office management systems prepare progress reports.*

OPEN HOUSE RESULTS

UR
H O M E   R E A L T Y

⟵ *Date and*
    address

Dear _____ :

This is just a short note to let you know about the open house for your home on [December 12].

We advertised the open house on [December 11 and 12] in [both the *Daily News* and the *Westside Sentinal*] and set up [directional signs, open house signs, and flags]. [We also sent out letters to (neighbors) and (visitors to other open houses).]

I registered [14] visitors to the open house. [1. Several additional visitors declined to register. 2. I was encouraged by the favorable comments by a number of the visitors.]

I will be contacting all the visitors to the open house within the next few days to ascertain their needs as well as their interest in your home.

[The market is relatively slow right now; therefore, I think we need to reexamine our strategy to excite buyers. I will call you in the next few days to discuss ways in which we can increase the desirability of your home.]

[I am very hopeful that, with our continued efforts, we will be able to find that special buyer for your home.]

Yours truly,

_____

Enclosure: ⟵ *Card*

CHANGE OF AGENTS

UR
H O M E   R E A L T Y

_____
_____ ◄------- *Date and*
                          address
_____
_____

Dear _____:

[Mr. Keith Swift] of our office will be taking over the primary responsibility of the sale of your home from [Ms. Karen Jones], who is no longer with our office. [Mr. Swift] will call you in the next few days to discuss our past and future efforts on your behalf.

If you have any questions at all, please do not hesitate to contact either [Mr. Swift] or me. I have enclosed one of [Mr. Swift's] cards.

Yours truly,

_____

Enclosure: ◄------ *New agent's card*

NOTE: *A better approach would be for the new agent to call the owners and arrange to meet with them to personally tell them he or she will be working with them on the sale of their home.*

PRICE ADJUSTMENT REQUEST—
NEW COMPARATIVE MARKET ANALYSIS

UR
_____

H O M E   R E A L T Y

_____

_____   ◄——— _Date and_
_____   _address_
_____

Dear _____:

Because of changes in the real estate marketplace, we have updated and enclosed a comparative market analysis indicating the current value of your home.

From the sales figures of comparable homes recently sold, as well as from the asking prices of similar homes that remain unsold, you will see that homes priced above the present market value are not selling. You will also see the necessity for a price adjustment to conform to market conditions. After all, the marketplace ultimately determines at what price a property will sell.

I have enclosed a [1. new listing 2. listing addendum] reflecting the current real estate market. Please sign and return [three] copies to our office.

I will be calling you within the next few days to answer any questions that you might have.

Yours truly,

_____

Enclosures: ◄——— _Card, comparative market analysis,_
                             listing addendum

NOTE: _It is better to blame the market rather than the home or the agency for the fact that a property has not sold. Never suggest "lowering" a price—the price is "adjusted" to reflect the market. Generally, a request to adjust a listing price should be made in person rather than by letter._

PRICE ADJUSTMENT REQUEST—
NEW LISTING AT LOWER PRICE

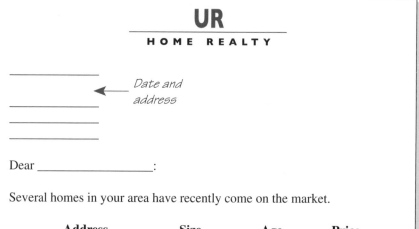

UR
H O M E   R E A L T Y

_____
_____   ← *Date and*
                    address
_____
_____

Dear _____:

Several homes in your area have recently come on the market.

Address	Size	Age	Price
[11 LaMont Circle]	[2,800 Sq. Ft.]	[4 Years]	[$465,000]
[74826 Crestview]	[2,650 Sq. Ft.]	[1 Year]	[$449,500]
[524 Adrian Way]	[2,790 Sq. Ft.]	[7 Years]	[$458,000]

[1. Listing information 2. A descriptive flyer] on each of the homes is included.

You will note that [two] of the listings are for [1. larger 2. newer] homes. In addition [one of the homes has a pool]. All [three] of these homes are priced lower than the price we have set for your home. Because of its price, by comparison your home will now appear to a buyer as being overpriced.

The market appears to be softening, which reduces the likelihood of selling your home at the list price of [$490,000]. If your home is to compete successfully in this market, I strongly suggest that the price be adjusted to [$459,000]. I have included a listing addendum reflecting this adjustment. Please sign and return [three] copies to this office.

Yours truly,

_____

Enclosures: ◄── *Card, property flyers, listing addendum*

NOTE: *This letter will make the owners realize that they are competing with other owners. It does not criticize the property; it places the blame on the market. Photos of the new listing can be shown by printing out the material from a Web site. Again, price adjustment requests should be made only by written communication when a personal face-to-face meeting is not possible.*

PRICE ADJUSTMENT REQUEST—
LENDER APPRAISAL BELOW LIST PRICE

UR
H O M E   R E A L T Y

_____ ←— _Date and_
_____   _address_
_____
_____

Dear _____:

I have just received the enclosed appraisal by [Midvale Savings and Loan] on your home.

Although I may not fully agree with this appraisal, it will nevertheless significantly affect prospective buyers, who will be reluctant to buy at a price above their lender's appraisal.

I therefore believe that it is in your best interest to adjust the price to reflect this appraisal. I have enclosed an addendum reflecting the new price. Please sign and return [two] copies.

[I will be calling you to answer any questions that you might have.]

Yours truly,

_____

Enclosures: ◄— _Card, appraisal report, listing addendum_

NOTE: _Never suggest "lowering" a price. The price is "adjusted" to reflect the lender's appraisal. Any request to adjust a listing price should be made in person whenever possible, rather than by letter._

PRICE ADJUSTMENT REQUEST—
PROPERTY ORIGINALLY PRICED ABOVE
COMPARATIVE MARKET ANALYSIS

UR
H O M E   R E A L T Y

_____

← *Date and*
    address

_____

_____

_____

Dear _____:

At the time we listed your home for sale at [111 Midvale Drive], our comparative market analysis indicated it had a market value of [$425,500]. Based on your decision as owner, the house was placed on the market at [$500,000].

Your home has now been on the market for [90] days. During this time we have advertised the property, called prospective buyers to discuss it, [held an open house,] posted photos and property details [including a virtual tour] on [three] Web sites, as well as to our multiple-listing service, which has [93] offices and [1,141] agents. Despite our best efforts, we have only shown your home to [seven] prospective buyers. [Several of those who have seen it expressed the opinion that your home, while desirable, is overpriced compared to other available properties.]

Therefore, in our professional judgment, the price should be adjusted to [$425,500], the figure that was indicated by our comparative market analysis. If you truly want to sell your home, I am certain that you will agree. I have enclosed a listing addendum that reflects this adjustment. Please sign and return [three] copies to my office.

I will be calling you to answer any questions that you might have.

Yours truly,

_____

Enclosures: ← *Card, comparative market analysis,*
                listing addendum

PRICE ADJUSTMENT REQUEST—
RAISE PRICE BASED ON MARKET COMPETITION

UR
H O M E   R E A L T Y

——————— ←— *Date and*
———————   *address*
———————
———————

Dear _____:

Recent sales indicate that [home] prices are escalating. We have therefore prepared a new comparative market analysis for your home at [1 1 1 Midvale Trail].

You'll see that it indicates our current asking price is too low. While the low price would likely mean a very quick sale, we feel we can get you a higher price within a reasonable period of time.

I have included a [1. listing addendum 2. new listing] reflecting a price adjustment to [$450,000]. Please sign and return [three] copies to this office.

I will call you in a few days to answer any questions that you might have.

Yours truly,

————————————

Enclosures: ◄— *Card, comparative market analysis,*
            listing addendum

NOTE: *A letter is not the preferred method of asking for a price adjustment. A letter should be used only when personal contact cannot be made.*

PRICE ADJUSTMENT REQUEST—FIXER-UPPER

UR
H O M E   R E A L T Y

_____
                 ← *Date and*
_____   *address*
_____
_____

Dear _____ :

The condition of your home at [55 Lynn Court] has made a sale difficult in our market. As you know, [1. the house needs decorating 2. the carpets need replacing 3. the home generally is showing the effects of its age]. Unless you are willing to extensively rehabilitate the property, I would like your permission to advertise your home as a fixer-upper. This type of ad has strong appeal to many buyers who are not afraid of hard work and who meet these challenges with enthusiasm.

To attract this type of buyer, a price adjustment would be necessary. I suggest [1. a price of ($279,500) 2. we offer the purchaser a renovation and decorating adjustment of ($40,000)]. I have enclosed a listing addendum that reflects this adjustment. Please sign and return [three] copies to this office.

I am confident that taking this approach will mean a timely sale of your property. I will be contacting you in the next few days to answer any questions that you might have.

Yours truly,

_____

Enclosures: ← *Card, listing addendum*

NOTE: *Again, the preferred method of communicating a request for a price adjustment is personal contact.*

An owner might find a "decorating adjustment" more palatable than a "price adjustment."

REQUEST FOR MINOR REPAIRS

UR
H O M E   R E A L T Y

_____
_____   ←—— *Date and*
                                  address
_____
_____

Dear _____:

Several prospective buyers who have visited your home have commented about the [1. broken porch railing 2. broken window panes]. Although this is not a major problem, it nevertheless presents a significant negative image to prospective buyers. We feel that it would be in your best interest to arrange for the necessary repair as soon as possible.

If you are unable to make the repair[s] yourself, I would be happy to recommend a [1. handyman 2. contractor] with whom I have had good experience in the past.

I will be calling you to answer any questions that you might have.

Yours truly,

_____

Enclosure: ←—— *Card*

REQUEST FOR LISTING EXTENSION

UR
H O M E   R E A L T Y

_____
_____   ◄— *Date and*
                          address
_____
_____

Dear _____:

The activity concerning your home has increased, and I feel certain we will be successful in arranging a sale. We have been making our utmost efforts on your behalf because we realize how important a sale is to you. During the last [six] months, we have placed numerous advertisements, placed photos of your home on [three] Web sites, held open houses, and provided information on your home to [our local real estate organization], which has [39] offices and [932] salespeople.

We want to not only continue our efforts but also increase them until we are successful. [1. To make our Web site listings stand out, we will be preparing a virtual tour of your home so prospective buyers can move from room to room, up and down, and left to right while viewing their computer. 2. We are scheduling open houses every week with greater newspaper coverage. 3. Your home will be featured as (*Home of the Week*) in the (*Midvale Homebuyers Guide*).]

I have enclosed an extension to our agency agreement. Please sign and return [three] copies so we can continue our efforts to consummate a sale without interruption. I will be contacting you in the next few days to answer any questions you might have and to discuss a marketing plan that will mean a successful sale.

Yours truly,

_____

Enclosures: ◄— *Card, agency agreement extension*

NOTE: *Ideally, a request for a listing extension should be made in person. It is easier to say no to a letter than it is to a person.*

The words "agency agreement" are more positive than "listing." "Agency" implies a benefit while "listing" implies payment of a fee.

LISTING EXTENDED—THANK YOU

UR

H O M E   R E A L T Y

_____
_____   ← *Date and*
                            address
_____
_____

Dear _____:

Thank you for the confidence you have shown in [UR Home Realty] in extending our agency agreement on your [home] at [27142 Lewis Lane].

I want you to know that we are dedicating our utmost efforts to the successful sale of your home. We realize how much a sale means to you. I feel certain that we will succeed in our quest for a buyer.

[Enclosed is an executed copy of the agency agreement extension.]

Yours truly,

_____

Enclosures: ←— *Card, signed agency agreement extension*

LISTING EXPIRED—THANK YOU FOR LISTING

UR
H O M E   R E A L T Y

Date and
address

Dear _____:

We regret that you have decided not to renew our agency agreement. However, I want to thank you for having given [UR Home Realty] the opportunity to serve as your sales agent.

[1. The market conditions were not favorable for a sale at the list price, although market conditions are now showing an improvement. 2. I feel a listing extension would result in a sale. However, with the present market, I suggest a listing range of from ($400,000) to ($475,000).]

Should you decide that you wish to use the services of [UR Home Realty] again, I have enclosed a new agency agreement. By signing and returning [three] copies to our office, you will once again be certain that we will use our best efforts to serve your interests. [The new agency agreement reflects our recommendations.]

[I will be calling you in the next few days to offer you some suggestions that should help in marketing your home.]

Yours truly,

_____

Enclosures: _Card, agency agreement_

PURCHASE OFFER TRANSMITTAL #1

UR

H O M E   R E A L T Y

FAX

Date: _____

To: _____

Attn: _____

From: _____

Pages w/cover: _____

Dear _____:

It took a lot of effort, but we were successful in obtaining the enclosed offer on your [home]. I believe it to be a reasonable offer because it provides you with [93 percent] of the offering price.

If you agree with me, please sign the enclosed purchase offer where indicated and fax the accepted purchase offer to me immediately. The buyers are not legally bound to this purchase offer until a signed acceptance is received. Until that time, they have the right to cancel their offer without penalty.

Please call me at [(800) 760-2111] as soon as you receive this fax so I can explain the entire offer and answer any questions that you might have.

Yours truly,

_____

Enclosures: ◄── *Card, offer to purchase*

NOTE: *Showing the offer as a percentage of the offering price tends to minimize the difference. Using the term "offering price" reminds the owner that this price is not sacred but is merely a hoped-for price.*

You create a sense of urgency by correctly pointing out that a buyer can back out prior to acceptance. Although sellers may refuse low offers, they don't like to allow the buyer to back out once an offer is made.

Whenever possible, offers should be presented in person. Fax presentations should be made only when face-to-face presentation is not practical.

When you take a listing from an out-of-the-area owner, you should ascertain the owner's fax number. If they don't have a fax, obtain the number that can be used at a local office service center such as Kinko's. Call or e-mail the owner that the fax has been sent.

PURCHASE OFFER TRANSMITTAL #2

UR
H O M E   R E A L T Y

FAX

Date: _____

To: _____   Attn: _____

From: _____   Pages w/cover: _____

Dear _____:

I have enclosed an offer we have received on your property at [5874 Greenview Lane]. The offer is not what we had hoped it would be. You now have the following three options:

1. Accept it. This would form a binding contract, and your home would be sold.

2. Reject it outright. This would end the negotiation process.

3. Make a counteroffer. You should realize that once a counteroffer is made, you can no longer accept the earlier offer, because that offer is considered to be dead. The buyers then have the option of accepting or rejecting your counteroffer.

If you feel you can't risk losing this buyer, I would recommend accepting the offer rather than making a counteroffer. If you can take the risk, I would recommend a counteroffer of [$430,000], although the amount of the counteroffer is your decision.

Besides the acceptance, which can be enacted by your signature, I have also prepared a counteroffer reflecting my recommendations. Please sign and fax me the applicable forms as soon as possible. Keep in mind that a buyer can withdraw an offer without penalty anytime prior to being notified of its acceptance.

Call me at my 800 number [(800) 670-2222] as soon as you receive this fax so that I can go through the offer with you and answer any questions you may have.

Yours truly,

_____

Enclosures: ◄—— *Card, offer to purchase, counteroffer*

NOTE: *See notes on prior fax transmittal letter.*

PURCHASE OFFER TRANSMITTAL / FULL PRICE

UR
H O M E   R E A L T Y

FAX

Date: _____

To: _____   Attn: _____

From: _____   Pages w/cover: _____

Dear _____:

I am proud to enclose a full-price purchase offer from [Janet Smith]. [The only deviation from your requirement is that (Ms. Smith) has requested a 60-day closing period.]

Before [1. he 2. she] is notified of your acceptance, [Ms. Smith] could conceivably revoke her offer; therefore, please sign and fax your acceptance, where indicated, immediately.

Please call me at [(800) 670-2212] when you receive this fax so that I can explain the offer and answer any questions you may have.

Yours truly,

_____

Enclosures: ◄—— *Card, offer to purchase*

NOTE: *An immediate notification that a fax is on its way should be made by phone or e-mail.*

POOR OFFER TRANSMITTAL

UR
H O M E   R E A L T Y

FAX   Date: _____

To: _____   Attn: _____

From: _____   Pages w/cover: _____

Dear _____:

As your agent, I am required to submit every offer received. I am therefore transmitting the enclosed purchase offer.

I recommend that rather than an outright rejection of this offer, we counter [1. with a price of ($419,000) 2. excluding the furnishings from the sale].

Although you have the right to accept the offer and form a binding contract, I hope that you will follow my advice; I do not think an acceptance of the offer as presented would be in your best interest.

Please call me at my 800 number, [(800) 760-2111], as soon as you receive this fax.

Yours truly,

_____

Enclosures: ◀—— *Card, offer to purchase, counteroffer*

NOTE: *If the offer revealed specific problems, such as dangerous clauses like subordination agreements, or if the offer involved unsecured notes or trades of property having questionable value, you should specifically point out these problems.*

SELLER NET PROCEEDS
ESTIMATE—AFTER OFFER

UR
H O M E   R E A L T Y

⟵ *Date and address*

Dear _____:

Enclosed is a seller net proceeds worksheet that I have prepared for your property, based on the purchase offer price of [**$419,000**].

I believe these figures are reliable but they are not guaranteed.

If you have any questions, please call me.

Yours truly,

_____

Enclosures: ⟵ *Card, seller net proceeds worksheet*

NOTE: *See page 132 for enclosure. Normally this would be covered when the offer was presented for acceptance.*

OFFER REJECTED

UR

H O M E   R E A L T Y

_____

⟵ *Date and*
address

_____

_____

_____

Dear _____ :

I'm very sorry the offer we received on your [1. home 2. property 3. lot] failed to meet your expectations. As your agents, we have a duty to present every offer received.

I want you to know that we will continue with our best efforts to sell your [1. home 2. property 3. lot], and we remain hopeful of an early success.

Yours truly,

_____

Enclosure: ⟵ *Card*

INFORMATION LETTER—STATUS OF SALE

To: [ ]

From: agent@urhomerealty.net

Subject: Financing Approved!

Dear _____:

Congratulations! [The financing has been approved] for [1. Janet Jones 2. the Joneses 3. the purchaser(s) of your (home)].

I will be contacting you within a few days to give you closing information.

Yours truly,

_____

Attachment: ◄—— *Card*

NOTE: *E-mail messages would be preferable to letters as to status of sale.*

REMOVAL OF CONTINGENCY

To: _____

From: agent@urhomerealty.net

Subject: Contingency Removed

Dear _____:

I am writing to notify you that [the Joneses] have signed the attached contingency release. Their purchase agreement now stands without the contingency [of obtaining a 6 percent loan for 80 percent of the purchase price].

[We should be able to close the sale by (November 1)].

Yours truly,

_____

Attachments: ◄—— *Card, contingency release*

NOTE: *See note on prior letter.*

FAILURE OF BUYER CONTINGENCY

UR
H O M E   R E A L T Y

_____   ← *Date and*
_____   *address*
_____
_____

Dear _____:

As I explained [1. in our phone conversation 2. in my e-mail message], [Mr. and Mrs. Brown] have been unable to [1. obtain financing 2. qualify] according to the contingency set forth in their purchase offer.

Please sign and return the enclosed release forms so that I can return their deposit in accord with our agreement.

We have resumed our sales efforts and are confident of success in selling your home.

Yours truly,

_____

Enclosures: ◄— *Card, release form, prepaid overnight delivery envelope*

NOTE: *When it appears a contingency will not be met, inform the owner immediately via phone or e-mail so that failure will not come as a shock. Be certain that the seller agrees to the return of the deposit before it is returned. Otherwise, a court could later decide that the failure to meet the contingency was the fault of the buyer. If this is the case, you could be held liable for the returned deposit.*

For a release, use either a standard form or have an attorney prepare one for you.

CLOSING DOCUMENTS TRANSMITTAL—
TO BUYER OR SELLER

UR
HOME REALTY

_____

_____   ←—— *Date and*
                            address
_____

_____

Dear _____:

Enclosed are the following documents for [1. your signature 2. both of your signatures]:

_____

_____

_____

_____

Please sign where indicated.

[Important: _____

_____

and _____

must be signed (in the presence of a notary public).]

Please return the documents as indicated by [10 June].

Yours truly,

_____

Enclosures: ←—— *Card, closing statement, deed, mortgage*

NOTE: *Ordinarily you should have buyer and seller come to your office or escrow office to sign documents. A letter would likely be used only where a party is not in the area. If mailed, use an overnight service that emphasizes the importance of the material, and include a similar prepaid return envelope.*

You should phone or e-mail the party that the material is on its way.

CLOSING STATUS—TO BUYER OR SELLER

UR
H O M E   R E A L T Y

_____
       ←   *Date and*
_____   *address*

_____
_____

Dear _____:

The closing of your [1. home sale 2. home purchase] [1. should be on schedule 2. is earlier than expected 3. is delayed because (state reasons); I will inform you as soon as this is resolved].

[1. We do not anticipate any problems with the closing. 2. If we encounter any problems, we will notify you immediately.]

If you have any questions, please contact me.

Yours truly,

_____

Enclosure: ◄— *Card*

NOTE: *If there is a problem or delay of any kind, the parties should preferably be notified immediately by phone or fax.*

NOTICE OF CLOSING

UR

H O M E   R E A L T Y

⟵ *Date and address*

Dear _____:

The closing for the sale of your home at [2713 Plymouth Street] will take place at [our Wells Street office at 9 A.M.] on [August 6]. [The seller must be present.] The following checklist may be helpful to you:

Seller's Checklist

❑ Notify the post office of your change of address.

❑ Notify magazines, credit card companies, banks, motor vehicle department, insurance companies, friends, and so on, of your address change.

❑ Cancel subscriptions to newspapers or let them know of your change of address.

❑ Cancel or arrange to transfer service contracts such as pest control, gardener, or water softener company.

❑ Cancel or transfer any homeowner's insurance coverage as of closing date.

❑ Disconnect or transfer utilities on final reading.
    ❑ Water
    ❑ Gas
    ❑ Electricity
    ❑ Phone
    ❑ Internet
    ❑ Cable TV
    ❑ Trash

(1)

NOTICE OF CLOSING *(continued)*

(2)

❏ Leave all warranties and manuals for appliances.

❏ Leave extra keys.

❏ Leave garage door openers, gate openers or cards, pool passes, as appropriate.

If you have any questions concerning the closing, please contact me.

Yours truly,

_____

Enclosure: ◄— *Card*

SETTLEMENT STATEMENT TRANSMITTAL

_____ **UR** _____

H O M E   R E A L T Y

_____

_____   ← *Date and*
                      address

_____

_____

Dear _____:

Enclosed is your check for [$207,812.69] as well as your settlement statement for the sale of your property at [77 Lynn Court].

We hope to be able to serve you for any future real estate needs.

Yours truly,

_____

Enclosures: ◄— *Card, check, settlement statement*

NOTE: *Normally, an independent escrow agent or an attorney would handle this. In some areas, brokers may act as escrow. Whenever possible, present checks in person. This gives you several opportunities: you can discuss an owner's future plans, ask for referrals, and request a testimonial letter.*

CLOSING STATEMENT QUESTION—BUYER OR SELLER

UR
H O M E   R E A L T Y

_____

← *Date and*
_____   *address*

_____

_____

Dear _____:

In regard to your [1. letter of (June 8) 2. telephone call on (June 8)], I have reviewed your closing statement for [1531 Rockwell Street].

[You are absolutely correct that an error was made, and I apologize for not discovering it. (1. I have enclosed a corrected statement and a check for ($30.50). 2. The escrow office will be sending you a corrected closing statement and a check.)]

[The document preparation charge was for preparation of the warranty deed and the second mortgage and note. The charge of ($40) is a reasonable charge for this service.]

[The charge for title insurance is based on (Paragraph 16) of the purchase contract whereby you agreed to provide this policy. It is also normal for the seller to pay for a standard policy of title insurance and the buyer to pay for any extended coverage desired.]

I will be calling you in the next few days to make certain that you fully understand the closing statement and to answer any other questions that you might have.

If you have any further questions or if I can be of service to you in any way, please do not hesitate to contact me.

Sincerely,

_____

Enclosure: ← *Card*

REQUEST FOR RETURN OF PERSONAL PROPERTY

UR

H O M E   R E A L T Y

_____

_____   ← _Date and address_

_____

_____

Dear _____ :

The [Smiths] are now in their new home and are delighted with it. [You certainly took excellent care of this fine home.]

We do have a minor problem: The [dining room ceiling fan] was not in the house when the [Smiths] took possession. Your movers might have inadvertently packed it. As you realize, [1. the purchase contract called for the ceiling fan to stay 2. the listing made a positive point of the ceiling fan remaining 3. the ceiling fan is regarded as a fixture, which must be left with the house unless agreed otherwise].

Please pack and return the [ceiling fan] to the [Smiths] as soon as practical. Thank you in advance for your prompt attention to this matter.

Yours truly,

_____

cc: [Smiths]

NOTE: _This is a diplomatic letter asking for the return of an item._

Ordinarily, a problem such as this occurs when the seller has not vacated at the time of closing so the "walk through" would not have revealed that the personal property was taken.

THANK YOU TO BUYER OR SELLER #1

UR

H O M E   R E A L T Y

_____
                    ←___ *Date and*
_____   *address*

_____
_____

Dear _____:

I would like to thank you for letting me serve you in the [1. sale 2. purchase] of your home. [1. I am certain your new home will bring your family much happiness. 2. Based on the current market, I believe that the (1. sale 2. purchase) was very advantageous to you.]

If I can be of any service to you in meeting your future real estate needs, do not hesitate to contact me. If you are happy with my services, I hope that you will recommend me to your friends.

Best wishes,

_____

Enclosure: ←___ *Card*

THANK YOU TO BUYER OR SELLER #2

UR
H O M E   R E A L T Y

_____

_____   ⟵ *Date and*
                        address

_____

_____

Dear _____:

Just a note to say "Thank you" [1. for entrusting the sale of your home to me
2. for allowing me to help you buy your new home].

All too often in today's rush of doing business, we forget to say "Thanks."
But not this time.

I have enjoyed fulfilling your needs. If I can ever do anything else for you,
please call on me.

Best Wishes,

_____

Enclosure: ⟵ *Card*

SERVICE EVALUATION—TO SELLER AFTER SALE

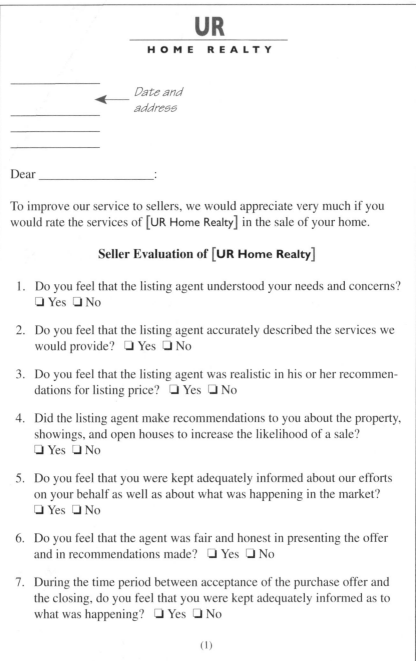

UR
H O M E   R E A L T Y

← *Date and address*

Dear _____:

To improve our service to sellers, we would appreciate very much if you would rate the services of [UR Home Realty] in the sale of your home.

Seller Evaluation of [UR Home Realty]

1. Do you feel that the listing agent understood your needs and concerns?
   ❏ Yes ❏ No

2. Do you feel that the listing agent accurately described the services we would provide? ❏ Yes ❏ No

3. Do you feel that the listing agent was realistic in his or her recommendations for listing price? ❏ Yes ❏ No

4. Did the listing agent make recommendations to you about the property, showings, and open houses to increase the likelihood of a sale?
   ❏ Yes ❏ No

5. Do you feel that you were kept adequately informed about our efforts on your behalf as well as about what was happening in the market?
   ❏ Yes ❏ No

6. Do you feel that the agent was fair and honest in presenting the offer and in recommendations made? ❏ Yes ❏ No

7. During the time period between acceptance of the purchase offer and the closing, do you feel that you were kept adequately informed as to what was happening? ❏ Yes ❏ No

(1)

SERVICE EVALUATION—TO SELLER AFTER SALE *(continued)*

---

(2)

8. Would you recommend our firm to a friend who needed to sell his or her home? ❑ Yes ❑ No

9. Can we use your name as a satisfied seller or allow other owners to see your evaluation of [UR Home Realty]? ❑ Yes ❑ No

10. We would appreciate your suggestions on how we can improve our services.

_____

_____

_____

_____

Please return this evaluation in the enclosed stamped envelope. Thank you for your time and consideration.

Yours truly,

[John Jones]
[Broker, UR Home Realty]

Enclosures: ◀—— *Card, stamped return envelope*

NOTE: *Negative responses identify weaknesses so that greater effort can be expended in the future. Positive responses provide you with an excellent listing tool.*

BUYER OR SELLER REQUEST FOR TESTIMONIAL LETTER

UR
H O M E   R E A L T Y

_____
_____ ← _Date and_
_____   _address_
_____

Dear _____:

I enjoyed working with you, and I am pleased that we were successful in
[1. the sale of your home 2. finding the house that has become your new home].

Many [1. sellers 2. buyers] are influenced by the experiences of others in
choosing a real estate agent to work with. If you could send me a letter
describing how you view my services, it would be of great help to me.

I thank you for your confidence in working with me and hope you think of
me should you have future real estate needs.

All the best,

_____

Enclosures: ← _Card, stamped return envelope_

THANK YOU FOR TESTIMONIAL LETTER

UR

H O M E   R E A L T Y

_____

_____ ⟵ *Date and*
_____   *address*

_____

_____

Dear _____:

Thank you *so* much for your kind letter. I am so pleased that you were happy with my services.

I will do my best to live up to the image you have given me in meeting any future real estate needs you might have. I want you to know that I am honored to have helped you in [1. buying 2. selling] your home.

All the best,

_____

Enclosure: ⟵ *Card*

NOTIFICATION TO SELLER OF REFERRAL

UR

H O M E   R E A L T Y

————————— ← *Date and*
—————————   *address*
—————————
—————————

Dear _____:

I am delighted that we were able to find a buyer for your home, but I am sad you will be leaving our community. One of the problems in real estate sales is that you really get to like people and then they are gone. However, I wish you great happiness in [Richmond].

To help you meet your housing needs, I have contacted [Tom Smith] of [Smith Realty] in [Richmond]. [(Tom) is a buyer's agent who has a duty to meet and protect the interests of buyers.] [Because I think (Tom) can help you, I gave (Tom) your e-mail address. He will be contacting you to ascertain your specific housing needs.] [I suggest you call (Tom) at ((800) 760-2222) to go over your specific housing needs.] [(Tom) can send you information and photos of available homes as well as provide Web site information so you can pre-search for the perfect home.] [Both our offices and (Smith Realty) are members of (Worldwide Referrals). It is a cooperative organization of over (1,800) real estate professionals concerned with meeting the relocation needs of homeowners.] I have also contacted the [Richmond] Chamber of Commerce, and they will be sending you area information and maps.

If I can ever be of service to you again, please don't hesitate to contact me.

Your friend,

_____

Enclosure: ← *Card*

BUYER LETTERS

PROPERTY INQUIRY LETTER #1

To: _____

From: | agent@urhomerealty.net

Subject: | Property Information

Dear _____:

The [111 Midvale Lane] property that you have inquired about offers a very special opportunity. Although you really must see the property in person to fully appreciate it, I have attached a descriptive sheet for you. You can also [1. view the property 2. take a virtual tour of the property] by visiting our Web site at [www.ur-home.net] and clicking on [Inventory #37A].

I will be calling you to answer any questions you may have and to tell you about several other properties that might be of interest to you.

Yours truly,

_____

Attachments: ◄—— *Card, property brief*

NOTE: *The purpose of the call would be to set up a definite time to show the property.*

If you have an e-mail address or fax number, these would be better methods of providing the information. Also consider an overnight service such as FedEx if you do not have an e-mail address. This helps to convey a sense of urgency.

PROPERTY INQUIRY LETTER #2

To: _____

From: | agent@urhomerealty.net

Subject: | Property Information

Dear _____:

I am very happy to send you the material that you requested on the [30 acres and 2 houses] advertised in the [Sunday Daily Ledger].

[I think you will get a better appreciation of this opportunity by viewing our Web site, (*www.ur-home.net*). You can click on (Inventory and check Homes with Acreage).]

[I have also included information on several similar properties that are available.] I will call you so we can arrange for you to view [1. this 2. these] rare opportunities.

Yours truly,

_____

Attachments: ◄——— *Card, property briefs*

NOTE: *The purpose of the call would be to set up a definite time to show the property.*

If you have an e-mail address or fax number, these would be better methods of providing the information. Also consider an overnight service such as FedEx if you do not have an e-mail address. This helps to convey a sense of urgency.

OUT-OF-AREA HOUSING INQUIRY

UR

H O M E   R E A L T Y

◄—— *Date and*
       address

Dear _____:

I will be happy to help you find a [3BR, 2-bath home with at least one acre of land] in the [Brookfield area] within the [$300,000–$350,000] price range you have indicated.

I have included descriptive information about some of the properties I think might interest you. Our Web site, [*www.ur-home.net*], will provide you with information, photos, and even virtual tours of these as well as additional properties.

I will be calling you to answer any questions you may have and to discuss any features you consider desirable for your future home, as well as to arrange a convenient time to show you our community and, hopefully, your next home.

Yours truly,

_____

Enclosures: ◄—— *Card, property briefs*

NOTE: *A preferred approach would be a phone call to discuss housing needs and to obtain an e-mail address to e-mail the information.*

OUT-OF-AREA BUYER—
NOTICE OF PROPERTIES OF INTEREST

To: _____

From: | agent@urhomerealty.net

Subject: | Available Properties

Dear _____:

I want to make you aware of [two] recently available properties that I feel will be of great interest to you.

[1823 West Winter Place is a 4-year-old Williamsburg Colonial with 4 BR, den, 3½ baths, and 3-car garage on a well-landscaped one-half acre site in a prestigious location. List price is $750,000, although I think there is some negotiation room.]

[17415 62nd Blvd. is an older Victorian of magnificent proportions that has been totally updated. There are 5BR, 4 full baths, and 2 half baths, separate 2BR, 1-bath suite above the 4-car garage, and it's set on over an acre. The property is in probate and is listed at $895,000 with any offer subject to court approval.]

I think it would be in your best interests to come to [Cleveland] at your earliest convenience to view these opportunities. [You can (1. view 2. tour) these properties on our Web site, (*www.ur-home.net*), by clicking on Inventory #47 and Inventory #51.]

Yours truly,

_____

NOTE: *This letter would be best as an e-mail because it expresses urgency. An e-mail also provides an opportunity to include a virtual tour. If none is available, you can create one yourself using a digital camera (check* www.visualtour.com, *one of several programs available).*

If a letter must be used, it should be sent via an overnight delivery service to express urgency.

It is essential that when you ask an out-of-area buyer to come quickly to view a property, you are reasonably certain the property will be what the buyer wants based on conversations and/or prior property showings. If the prospective buyer is not interested in the property, your credibility will suffer and you could lose a valued prospective buyer.

REQUEST FOR BUYER INFORMATION

To:	
From:	agent@urhomerealty.net
Subject:	Buyer Confidential Information Form

Dear _____:

To best meet your housing needs, I would appreciate if you could complete the attached Prospective Buyer Confidential Information Form.

Although some of the questions may seem personal, we need this information to understand your needs and to prequalify you for any required loan. This is really the first step toward locating a new home for you and your family. Thank you!

Yours truly,

_____

Attachments: ◄─── *Card, prospective buyer confidential information form*

NOTE: *An e-mail and the following form as an attachment would be appropriate in lieu of a letter.*

PROSPECTIVE BUYER
CONFIDENTIAL INFORMATION FORM

Prospective Buyer Confidential Information

Name(s): _____   Phone: _____

E-mail: _____   Fax: _____

Address: _____

Size of family: _____

Names and ages of children or other dependents living with you:

_____ ; _____ ;

_____ ; _____ ;

_____ ; _____

Initial contact with this firm was motivated by (advertisement, sign, referral, etc.): _____

Present address: _____

How long at above address? _____

Do you presently own your own home? ❏ Yes ❏ No

If yes, must you sell before you buy? ❏ Yes ❏ No

If yes, is your present home currently listed for sale? ❏ Yes ❏ No
With: _____

Your reason(s) for buying a new home: _____
_____
_____

How long have you been looking for a new home? _____

Have you found any home that you like? ❏ Yes ❏ No
If yes, why didn't you purchase? _____

Areas or locations that are of special interest to you: _____
_____
_____

Why? _____
_____
_____

(1)

PROSPECTIVE BUYER
CONFIDENTIAL INFORMATION FORM *(continued)*

(2)

Do you currently own all of your own appliances (stove, refrigerator, washer/dryer)? _____

What features do you like about your present home? _____

_____

_____

Why? _____

_____

_____

Do you have a pet? ❏ Yes ❏ No   What kind?

_____

Do you have any special needs such as handicapped-accessible? ❏ Yes ❏ No

Describe these requirements: _____

_____

What are your hobbies or special interests? _____

_____

Have you qualified for or been turned down for a home loan within the past year? _____

If you qualified for a loan, what was the name of the firm and loan amount?

_____

Approximate monthly gross income (before taxes and other deductions):
$ _____

Total monthly payments on long-term debt (one year or more revolving credit accounts plus car, etc.): $ _____

What are you willing to invest toward a down payment on a home?
$ _____

This form will be kept in a confidential prospective buyer file by

[UR Home Realty]
[(318) 807-2136]

NOTE: *This form could be used as a mailing or e-mail attachment or could be delivered in person to determine housing needs and financial qualification.*

PROSPECTIVE BUYER—NEW LISTING

To: [   ]

From: agent@urhomerealty.net

Subject: New Listing

Dear _____:

[I was unable to reach you by phone, but I wanted to let you know that] we
have just accepted a new listing that I believe is exactly what you have
been looking for. I want you to see this very special home before
it is advertised to the general public.

Please call me at once. I wouldn't want you to miss this opportunity!

Yours truly,

_____

NOTE: *While preferable as an e-mail message, a letter should be used if the
party does not have an e-mail address. Send this letter special delivery or
overnight delivery. This letter creates a sense of urgency and sets a buying,
rather than looking, mood. No information is given because if it included anything buyers considered negative, they would not be eager to see the property.
You can continue the tone of urgency by asking prospective buyers if they
can take time off from work to see it. If they like the house, they will be happy
they did. Warning: Be reasonably certain that this is the house for your clients,
or your credibility could be damaged.*

E-MAIL ALERT

To:	
From:	agent@urhomerealty.net
Subject:	E-mail Alert—New Property on Market

Dear _____:

The [4-year-old, 3BR, 2½ bath, center hall Colonial] at [6722 Edgemont] in [Orchard Ridge] has come on the market today. It is listed at [$347,900].

[Photo and Details]

Please reply to this message if you would like to be the first to see this fine property.

If any of your friends would like to receive these e-mail alerts, have them e-mail or call me.

[UR Home Realty]
[(760) 200-8888]
[John Davis]
[jdavis@ur-home.net]

NOTE: *Whenever you receive an inquiry about property, you should ask the prospective buyers if they would like to receive e-mail alerts of new listings that meet their criteria as soon as they are received and before the property is advertised to the general public. Most callers will like to have this advantage and will readily provide their e-mail addresses.*

PROSPECTIVE BUYER—PRICE REDUCTION

UR

H O M E   R E A L T Y

_____   ← Date and
_____   address
_____
_____

Dear _____:

The house you liked so much in [Elmside], the one with [the huge fireplace and the fruit trees in the backyard], has just been reduced in price. The original price set by the owners was [$269,500], but they have reduced this to [$237,000], a net reduction of [$32,500].

This reduction should result in a very quick sale. Because I would hate to see anyone else get this exceptional buy, I think you should take another look at this property. I will call you to arrange a showing of this home and another new listing that I think will interest you.

Yours truly,

_____

Enclosure: ◄—— Card

NOTE: _While an initial phone call or e-mail would be preferable to a letter, this letter would be appropriate for a prospective buyer living outside the area who has been unreachable by phone and who has no e-mail address. Send this letter if the prospects indicated mild interest. The mention of the other home is a final hook to set up the showings._

**COVER LETTER, OFFER TO PURCHASE
(OUT-OF-AREA BUYER)**

UR

H O M E   R E A L T Y

_____

_____ ←— *Date and
address*

_____

_____

Dear _____:

In accord with our telephone discussion on [Wednesday, October 8], I have prepared a purchase offer for the property at [111 Midvale Lane] as you directed. The purchase offer reflects your offering price of [$265,000] and it includes [1. terms 2. items that vary from the listing, and any special conditions].

Please sign and return [three] copies of the purchase agreement to me as soon as possible along with [your deposit check for $10,000], [which will be held uncashed until the offer is accepted]. If the offer is not accepted, your deposit will be returned to you in full.

If the owners accept your offer, I believe that you will have made an exceptionally fine purchase. [Even at the list price, I think this home is an excellent buy.]

Call me at [1-800-621-1121] as soon as you receive this package so that I can go over the purchase offer with you and answer any questions you may have.

Yours truly,

_____

Enclosures: ←— *Card, offer to purchase*

NOTE: *The letter should be sent by overnight delivery service such as FedEx, and a paid envelope should be included for similar return service.*

   If time is a critical factor, you could fax the form and the buyer could fax the signed offer back and send the earnest money as a wire transfer.

NOTIFICATION OF OFFER ACCEPTANCE

To: _____

From: agent@urhomerealty.net

Subject: Offer Accepted!

Dear _____:

I am pleased to inform you that your offer for the purchase of the property at [55 Chestnut Street] has been accepted without qualification. Attached is the signed acceptance.

[As your agent], I will work with you throughout the closing process.

I congratulate you on your wonderful purchase.

Sincerely,

_____

Attachments: ⟵— *Card, executed purchase agreement*

NOTE: *The preferred method of notification is in person. If this is not possible, make the notification by phone or e-mail indicating that the acceptance has been mailed via an overnight delivery service. Generally, acceptance does not take place until delivered to offeror, and mailing constitutes delivery.*

REJECTION OF OFFER—NO COUNTEROFFER
(RECOMMEND NEW FULL-PRICE OFFER)

UR

H O M E   R E A L T Y

_____

◄──── *Date and*
address

_____

_____

_____

Dear _____ :

[Mr. and Mrs. Jones] have indicated that they are unable to accept your offer to purchase their [home]. Although they would very much like to sell to you, they feel that the price they had set is more than reasonable based on the current real estate marketplace.

Because I feel very strongly that this [home] meets your needs better than any other [home] available and that the price asked is favorable, I have enclosed a new offer form reflecting that price.

If you wish to be the owner of this wonderful [home], please sign and return [three] copies of the offer in the envelope provided. [It would be unfortunate to lose this fine opportunity for a difference of only about five percent.]

I will call you to answer any questions that you might have.

Yours truly,

_____

P.S. Keep in mind that long after the price has been forgotten you will be enjoying the [1. amenities 2. advantages] of this fine [home].

Enclosures: ◄──── *Card, offer to purchase*

NOTE: *If at all possible, prospective buyers should be immediately notified by phone, e-mail, or in person of a rejection of their offer. A personal notification would be preferable.*

If a phone call or e-mail was used, start the letter with, "In accord with [1. our telephone discussion 2. my e-mail of October 20] *. . . "*

This letter should be sent by an overnight service with paid return envelope.

NOTICE TO BUYER OF SELLER COUNTEROFFER
(RECOMMEND ACCEPTANCE)

UR
H O M E   R E A L T Y

_____ ◄── _Date and_
_____   _address_

_____
_____

Dear _____:

[Mr. and Mrs. Smith], the owners of the property at [8712 Mayville Lane], have presented a counter to your offer to purchase their home. The changes they have made are as follows:

1. [Price to be $529,000 rather than the $499,000 price that you offered.]

2. [Closing to be in 60 days rather than the 30 days that you indicated.]

[At the time of your offer, I indicated that a price of ($499,000) was probably a little low based on comparables.] [The list price of ($559,000) was not unreasonable but your offer has resulted in a counteroffer giving you a ($30,000) reduction from the list price.]

I believe that the counteroffer of [$529,000] is still an excellent purchase opportunity and recommend your acceptance of the counteroffer.

Please sign and fax a copy of your acceptance of the counteroffer to me at [(760) 200-8888] and mail [three] copies of the signed acceptance to me.

Until this counteroffer is accepted, the owners have the right to revoke this counteroffer.

Sincerely,

_____

Enclosures: ◄── _Card, three copies of counteroffer,_
addressed prepaid envelope

NOTE: _If presentation is not possible in person, the buyers should be notified by phone or e-mail of the counteroffer. They could then fax acceptance of the stated_ changes (check with your attorney as to fax acceptances in your state). As an alternative approach, you could send this letter by fax or an overnight service.

By showing the buyers that their negotiations gave them a discount from the list price, you increase the likelihood of acceptance.

BUYER PURCHASE COST ESTIMATE

UR

H O M E   R E A L T Y

_____

_____ ← *Date and*
address
_____

_____

Dear _____ :

Enclosed is our Buyer Cost Estimate Worksheet. While we believe that the estimates are reasonably reliable, they are not guaranteed.

If you have any questions, please call me.

Yours truly,

_____

Enclosures: ◄—— *Card, buyer cost estimate worksheet*

NOTE: *The Buyer Cost Estimate Worksheet is on page 193.*

BUYER COST ESTIMATE WORKSHEET

UR
H O M E   R E A L T Y

Buyer Cost Estimate
Prepared for [John and Sara Smith]

Property: _____

Costs		Credits	
Purchase price	$ _____	Down payment	$ _____
Loan costs		Loans being assumed	($ _____)
Appraisal fee	$ _____	Seller financing	($ _____)
Origination costs	$ _____	Taxes (prorated)	($ _____)
Miscellaneous fees	$ _____	Other	$ _____
Impound account	$ _____	**Total credits**	$ _____
Buyer broker fee	$ _____		
Inspection costs	$ _____		
Insurance	$ _____		
Taxes (prorated)	$ _____		
Title insurance/abstracts	$ _____		
Attorney fees/escrow	$ _____		
Miscellaneous costs	$ _____		
Total costs	$ _____		
Total credits	($ _____)		
	$ _____	To be financed or paid at closing	

WAIVER OF CONTINGENCY REQUEST

UR
H O M E   R E A L T Y

_____

← *Date and*
_____   *address*

_____

_____

Dear _____ :

Your offer-to-purchase agreement dated [11 August 2005] was contingent on [the sale of your home on Doyle Street].

The purchase contract provides that if a subsequent written offer is accepted that is contingent on your rights, you shall have [seven days] to waive the contingencies set forth in your offer. You are hereby notified that a subsequent offer has been received and accepted. Unless the seller shall have received notice by [14 September] that you have waived your contingencies, your offer shall terminate and become void, and your earnest money deposit will be returned to you. You are also advised that such notification must be prompt.

A contingency release form is included for your signature. If you wish to waive the contingencies in your purchase offer, please sign where indicated and fax the release to me.

If you have any questions, please contact me immediately.

Yours truly,

_____

Enclosures: ← *Card, contingency release form*

cc: [Owner]

NOTE: *If the buyer cannot be personally contacted, the buyer should be notified immediately by phone and the letter and contingency release form preferably should be made by e-mail or fax. The form should then be returned by fax. If mailed as a letter, it should be sent by express carrier, unless the offer prescribes another manner for delivery of notices.*

PROBLEM WITH A CONTRACT CONDITION—
BUYER OR SELLER

UR
H O M E   R E A L T Y

_____
_____   ⟵ *Date and*
                   address
_____
_____

Dear _____:

As we agreed in our telephone discussion on [July 25], your purchase contract for the [1. purchase 2. sale] of [11475 Wedgewood Way] requires that [1. an 80 percent loan commitment 2. roof replacement] be [1. obtained 2. completed] by [August 1].

[1. You indicated 2. It is my understanding] that the above condition has not yet been fulfilled. You therefore are at risk of the [1. buyer 2. seller] declaring you to be in default of your agreement, [which could result in damages].

If there is any problem fulfilling the required condition, [or if I can be of any help to you], please contact me immediately so I can work with you toward a satisfactory solution.

Yours truly,

_____

Enclosure: ⟵ *Card*

cc: [1. Buyer 2. Seller]

NOTE: *After a phone call, a letter should be used to document the problem. If there appears to be a problem, the other party should, of course, be notified.*

BUYER FAILED CONTINGENCY

_____

UR
H O M E   R E A L T Y

_____
_____   ◄—— *Date and*
_____   *address*
_____

Dear _____ :

Your offer dated [June 1, 2005] to purchase the property at [2736 Wright Road in Newton Heights] was contingent on [your obtaining a $300,000 loan with $30,000 down by July 15]. You were unable to [obtain the required financing and have indicated that you are unable to waive the contingency]. Therefore, in accord with your purchase offer, your offer has become null and void. With the concurrence of the owners, I am enclosing [UR Home Realty] trust account check No. [2933] in the amount of [$5,000], representing the full return of your earnest money deposit made with your offer to purchase.

If you have any questions or if I can serve you in any way, please contact me.

Yours truly,

_____

Enclosures: ◄—— *Card, check*

cc: [Owner's name]

NOTE: *This letter provides a written record of what should have been discussed by phone. Obtain owner's concurrence in writing before earnest money is returned because of a failed contingency.*

INFORMATION TO NEW OWNER

UR
HOME REALTY

_____
_____ ⟵ *Date and*
_____   *address*
_____
_____

Dear _____:

To aid you in getting established in your new home, we have included a list of phone numbers for utility hook-ups, [cable TV], [trash pickup], and [newspapers], as well as some general area information that we believe will be useful to you. If [UR Home Realty] can be of any further assistance to you, or if you know anyone with real estate needs, please contact me.

Wishing you a great life in your new home,

_____

Enclosures: ⟵ *Card, lists, general information*

NOTE: *In addition to phone numbers, consider area maps, school information, information on all area houses of worship, bus information, and so on. Your local chamber of commerce office probably can supply you with a large packet of information for the new resident.*

INFORMATION ON UTILITIES AND SERVICES

UR

H O M E   R E A L T Y

_____   ← *Date and*
_____   *address*
_____
_____

Dear _____:

For your information, here are a few numbers that will help when you move
into your new home:

Telephone service _____

Internet service providers _____

Gas connection _____

Electrical service _____

Water _____

Cable TV _____

Newspaper _____

Trash service _____

School registration _____

Emergency Numbers

    Fire _____

    Police _____

    Ambulance _____

    [Other] _____

If you like, I would be happy to give you my recommendations for everything
from an auto mechanic to a [hairstylist].

Sincerely,

_____

Enclosure: ← *Card*

SCHOOL REGISTRATION INFORMATION

UR

H O M E   R E A L T Y

_____ ← _Date and_
_____   _address_
_____
_____

Dear _____:

Just a quick note to let you know that you can register [Judy and Bobby] for [Midvale School starting July 10].

By registering early, you will avoid having to rush after you move into your new home. I am certain that you will have plenty of other things to keep you busy.

Best regards,

_____

Enclosure: ◀— _Card_

INSURANCE SOLICITATION

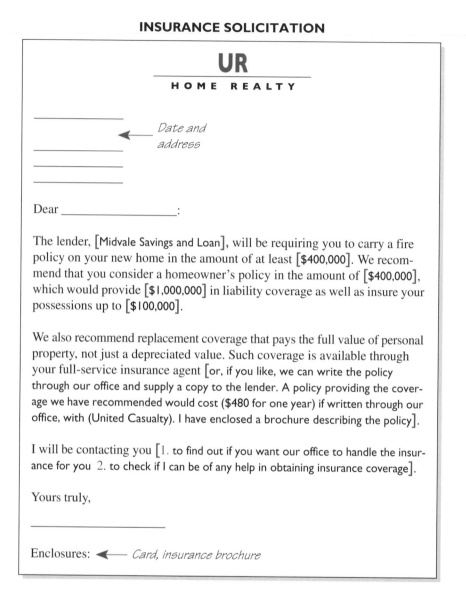

UR
H O M E   R E A L T Y

⟵ *Date and address*

Dear _____ :

The lender, [Midvale Savings and Loan], will be requiring you to carry a fire policy on your new home in the amount of at least [$400,000]. We recommend that you consider a homeowner's policy in the amount of [$400,000], which would provide [$1,000,000] in liability coverage as well as insure your possessions up to [$100,000].

We also recommend replacement coverage that pays the full value of personal property, not just a depreciated value. Such coverage is available through your full-service insurance agent [or, if you like, we can write the policy through our office and supply a copy to the lender. A policy providing the coverage we have recommended would cost ($480 for one year) if written through our office, with (United Casualty). I have enclosed a brochure describing the policy].

I will be contacting you [1. to find out if you want our office to handle the insurance for you 2. to check if I can be of any help in obtaining insurance coverage].

Yours truly,

_____

Enclosures: ⟵ *Card, insurance brochure*

BUYER—FINAL INSPECTION

UR
H O M E   R E A L T Y

_____
_____   ◄—— *Date and*
_____   *address*
_____

RE: [Address]

Dear _____:

In accord with your purchase agreement, I have arranged for you to conduct a final [walk-through inspection] of the property on [Tuesday, September 23, at 10 A.M.].

[1. I will meet you at the property. 2. You can of course bring a professional inspector with you.] If for any reason you are not going to be available at this time, please contact me as soon as possible.

Yours truly,

_____

Enclosure: ◄—— *Card*

NOTE: *Purchase contracts customarily provide for the purchaser to have a professional inspection and may provide for a final walk-through inspection.*

BUYER/SELLER NOTICE OF SETTLEMENT CONFERENCE

_____ **UR** _____

H O M E   R E A L T Y

_____
_____ ← *Date and*
_____   *address*
_____
_____

Dear _____:

The settlement conference for your [1. sale 2. purchase] of [111 Midvale Lane] has been scheduled for [June 1, 2005] at [55 Sycamore Place, Suite 3301].

[All (1. buyers 2. sellers) must attend so they can sign the (1. mortgage 2. deed).]

[1. Please bring a cashier's check in the amount of ($39,528). 2. Please see the enclosed statement.]

I am glad that we have been able to fulfill your needs [and I look forward to seeing you at the closing].

Best regards,

_____

Enclosures: ← *Card, settlement statement*

NOTE: *The trend is for settlements to be handled by an independent escrow without buyers or sellers being present.*

CLOSING STATEMENT TRANSMITTAL

UR
H O M E   R E A L T Y

_____ ⟵ *Date and*
_____   *address*
_____
_____

Dear _____:

Enclosed is a copy of the closing statement for your [1. sale of 2. purchase of] [6160 Jupiter Lane].

[I am certain that you will enjoy many happy years in your new home.] If you or your friends have any future real estate needs, I hope that you will think of me.

Sincerely,

_____

Enclosures: ⟵ *Card, closing statement*

NOTE: *If an escrow is used, they would send out the closing statement.*

SERVICE EVALUATION—BUYER AFTER SALE

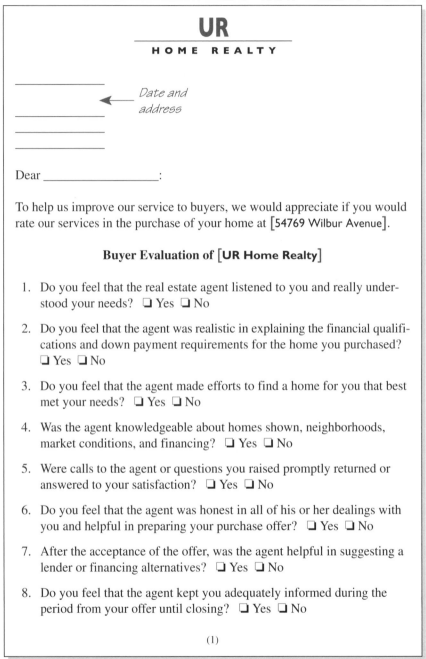

UR

H O M E   R E A L T Y

⟵ *Date and address*

Dear _____ :

To help us improve our service to buyers, we would appreciate if you would rate our services in the purchase of your home at [54769 Wilbur Avenue].

Buyer Evaluation of [UR Home Realty]

1. Do you feel that the real estate agent listened to you and really understood your needs? ❑ Yes ❑ No

2. Do you feel that the agent was realistic in explaining the financial qualifications and down payment requirements for the home you purchased? ❑ Yes ❑ No

3. Do you feel that the agent made efforts to find a home for you that best met your needs? ❑ Yes ❑ No

4. Was the agent knowledgeable about homes shown, neighborhoods, market conditions, and financing? ❑ Yes ❑ No

5. Were calls to the agent or questions you raised promptly returned or answered to your satisfaction? ❑ Yes ❑ No

6. Do you feel that the agent was honest in all of his or her dealings with you and helpful in preparing your purchase offer? ❑ Yes ❑ No

7. After the acceptance of the offer, was the agent helpful in suggesting a lender or financing alternatives? ❑ Yes ❑ No

8. Do you feel that the agent kept you adequately informed during the period from your offer until closing? ❑ Yes ❑ No

(1)

SERVICE EVALUATION—BUYER AFTER SALE *(continued)*

(2)

9. Would you recommend the services of the agent to a friend who wanted to buy a home? ❑ Yes ❑ No

10. Can we show this evaluation to other prospective buyers? ❑ Yes ❑ No

11. If requested, would you be willing to write a short testimonial letter as to your relationship with [UR Home Realty]? (This letter would be shown to prospective buyers.) ❑ Yes ❑ No

12. May we phone you in the future for information about your neighborhood and referrals? ❑ Yes ❑ No

13. Any additional comments: _____
_____
_____

Signature _____

Please return this evaluation in the enclosed stamped envelope. Thank you very much for your assistance.

Yours truly,

_____

[UR Home Realty]

Enclosure: ◄—— *Card*

NOTE: *Buyers usually develop a rapport with the selling agent. Because this is an evaluation of that agent, you will receive many "Yes" responses. With the buyers' approvals, an agent can show these evaluations to prospective buyers during the qualification process. Positive evaluations help sell the agent as someone who is very helpful to buyers.*

If buyers indicate they are willing to provide a testimonial letter, a letter should be requested. A folder of such letters can be very persuasive in obtaining buyer agency.

Permission to phone may provide an exception to the Do-Not-Call Registry rules.

NOTICE TO APPLY FOR HOMEOWNER TAX EXEMPTION

_____

UR
_____   _____
H O M E   R E A L T Y

_____
                    ←—— *Date and*
_____   *address*

_____

_____

Dear _____:

[California] offers a special property tax exemption for owner-occupied homes. You must, however, apply for this exemption by [April 15] for the [2005] tax year. I have enclosed [1. information on applying for the exemption 2. an exemption application] for your convenience. I would feel terrible if you did not receive the benefits you are entitled to. If you have any questions, please contact me.

Sincerely,

_____

Enclosures: ←—— *Card, tax exemption application*

_____

NOTE: *In many states, a resident homeowner is entitled to special tax treatment, but the homeowner must apply for it. In many areas, the escrow process will include the homeowner tax exemption applications.*

INSURANCE SOLICITATION—MORTGAGE INSURANCE

UR
H O M E   R E A L T Y

⟵ *Date and
address*

Dear _____:

I hope that you are enjoying your lovely new home. You might be interested in the enclosed brochure. It concerns a mortgage insurance policy that will pay off your mortgage if you die or will make the payments for you if you become disabled. Because of your concern for your family, please consider this plan.

The premiums on your mortgage at your age of [39] come to only [$24] a [month], and the payments are guaranteed to remain the same for the life of the loan.

I will be calling you in a few days to answer any questions you might have concerning this low-cost family protection.

Sincerely,

_____

Enclosures: ⟵ *Card, insurance brochure*

NOTE: *If you sell mortgage insurance, a good time to sell is after the home sale has been closed. Before the sale, buyers are concerned about all the expenses of closing, and they are more reluctant to take on new debt. Mortgage insurance is actually decreasing term life insurance.*

BUYER WHO PURCHASED THROUGH ANOTHER BROKER

UR
H O M E   R E A L T Y

◄—— *Date and*
address

Dear _____:

Congratulations! I was very happy to learn that you had found the [home] that fulfills your needs. Although I am sorry I was unable to locate that [special home] for you, I do wish you happiness in your new [home]. From what I know of the area, I am certain that you made a wise choice.

If you need real estate assistance in the future, I hope you will think of me. I am ready to give my best efforts on your behalf.

Sincerely,

_____

Enclosure: ◄—— *Card*

NOTE: *This letter reestablishes the relationship for future referrals or dealings. Otherwise, the buyers might avoid the agent because they believe he or she is angry with them for going elsewhere.*

The buyer might have developed a better rapport with the agent who failed to make the sale than the successful agent.

ANNIVERSARY OF PURCHASE

UR
H O M E   R E A L T Y

_____

_____   ←········ *Date and*
                                  address

_____

_____

Dear _____:

Although it is hard to realize, we are celebrating your anniversary this week! On [June 1], it will be exactly [one] year since [1. I sold you your home 2. you purchased your home through our office]. I hope that your home has been good to you in those years; [I know that it has certainly appreciated in value].

I will call you in a few days to ask for your help in identifying any of your friends who might need real estate services.

Happy anniversary!

_____

Enclosure: ◄─── *Card*

NOTE: *A call after 18 months would require that the party not be listed on the Do-Not-Call Registry or that you obtained written permission to call for referrals.*

BREACH OF CONTRACT AND OTHER LETTERS OF CONFLICT

Note: In most cases, the broker's first action when a conflict appears to be present should be a phone call. A phone call can mean immediate resolution of a conflict.

RELEASE OF LISTING

___UR___

H O M E   R E A L T Y

_____

_____ ← *Date and*
                     address

_____

_____

Dear _____:

You have indicated [by your letter of April 3] that you no longer wish [UR Home Realty] to represent you in the sale of [your home] at [2137 Northbridge Road].

Therefore, I have enclosed a release form that releases you and [UR Home Realty] from any and all obligations under [the Exclusive-Right-to-Sell Listing dated (March 1, 2005),] and cancels said listing agreement.

Please endorse two copies of the enclosed release [where indicated] and return them to me in the enclosed stamped envelope. I will then sign them and return a copy to you.

I regret that we were unable to get your property under contract. Please call us if you have any questions or if we can be of service in any way in the future.

Yours truly,

_____

Enclosures: ← *Card, release*

NOTE: *Use a listing release form either prepared by your attorney or one endorsed by your local professional real estate organization. Do not attempt to draft your own legal document.*
Many brokers prefer a release to a lawsuit for damages.

**RESPONSE TO OWNER OR ATTORNEY—
CANCELLATION OF LISTING**

UR
H O M E   R E A L T Y

_____

◄—— *Date and
address*

_____

_____

_____

Dear _____:

I have received your [letter] of [December 1, 2005], in which you unilaterally canceled the listing agreement of [October 12, 2005], on the property located at [78153 Towne Avenue].

[1. We have worked diligently toward the sale of said property and have been meeting our contractual obligations. Therefore, under Paragraph (16A) of the listing, demand is hereby made for the agreed cancellation fee of ($15,000).]

[2. Although we have worked diligently toward the sale of the property, we do understand the unique circumstances involved and are willing to meet with you in the hope of reaching a mutually satisfactory settlement.]

[I will be contacting you so that we can resolve this matter.]

Yours truly,

_____

Enclosure: ◄—— *Card*

NOTE: *Because of the time and cost involved in legal action, as well as the hard feelings it generates, it is generally preferable to mutually agree to a settlement.*

DEMAND FOR COMMISSION—
OWNER'S ACTION PREVENTS SALE

UR
H O M E   R E A L T Y

_____
_____   ← *Date and*
                         address
_____

_____

Dear _____:

Pursuant to our [Exclusive-Agency-Listing Agreement] on your property at
[18 Westwood Court], our office was successful in obtaining an offer on said
property. You accepted this offer to purchase on [January 14, 2006].

A sale was not concluded because you [1. were unable to clear title 2. failed
to comply with the condition that the roof be replaced 3. refused to complete
the transaction].

Our office has fully complied with the terms of said listing agreement in
obtaining a buyer who was ready, willing, and able to buy under the price
and terms you agreed to.

I will be calling you [to arrange a meeting] to clarify why the sale failed and
to settle any obligations.

Yours truly,

_____

Enclosure: ◄─── *Card*

NOTE: *This letter states the facts as you know them. You are seeking to meet
with the owner and reach a settlement.*
*If another office procured the buyer, the broker for that office should be
involved.*
*If an agreement cannot be worked out, then you should consider turning the
matter over to an attorney.*

DEMAND FOR COMMISSION—
OWNER REFUSES FULL-PRICE OFFER

UR
H O M E   R E A L T Y

_____
_____   ◄— *Date and*
_____   *address*
_____

Dear _____:

Under the terms of our [Exclusive-Listing Agreement] dated [April 12, 2005], [UR Home Realty] worked diligently to obtain a buyer for your property at [6714 Freeport Avenue].

On [August 1, 2005], we presented you with a full-price offer of [$529,000] in full accord with the terms specified in the listing agreement. The buyer, [Jane Jones], was ready, willing, and able to complete the purchase.

You responded to said offer by [1. refusing to sell 2. countering the offer with a price greater than the listing price].

Under [Paragraph 6] of our agreement, [UR Home Realty] is entitled to the commission of [$31,740] based on your refusal to sell under the terms of our agreement.

I will be calling you in the next few days [to arrange to meet with you] in order to discuss our future relationship and obligations.

Yours truly,

_____

Enclosure: ◄— *Card*

NOTE: *A settlement might involve a payment of money and/or a new listing at a different price, terms, and/or commission.*

If another broker procured the full-price offer, then that broker should be involved in any settlement agreement.

If the matter cannot be resolved to your satisfaction, legal services should be considered.

OWNER REMOVES PROPERTY FROM MARKET—
LISTING IS NOT CANCELLED

UR
H O M E   R E A L T Y

_____
_____   ◄—— *Date and*
_____   *address*
_____

Dear _____:

By your request, we will no longer advertise or show your [home] at [38217 Lilac Avenue] for sale. We will also take down our sign and remove the property from our multiple-listing service and all Internet sites.

However, the listing agreement, as agreed, will remain in full force and effect. If you or anyone else sells the [house] while our agreement is in effect, we will be entitled to our full compensation under the terms of our [Exclusive-Right-to-Sell listing].

If you later decide to sell your home, we hope that you will consider the services and courtesy we have shown you.

Yours truly,

_____

Enclosure: ◄—— *Card*

NOTE: *This is not a release. A release from the listing would allow the owner to sell without paying any commission. This letter offers you protection if the owner asks to be released with the intention of avoiding commission payment because he or she has secretly located a buyer.*

This letter should be sent registered mail, return receipt requested.

COMMISSION DUE—
OWNER REMOVES PROPERTY FROM MARKET

UR
H O M E   R E A L T Y

_____
_____ ⟵ *Date and*
                 address
_____
_____

Dear _____ :

In accord with an Exclusive-Agency agreement dated [May 14, 2005], [UR Home Realty] has been diligent in searching for a buyer for your property at [197641 141st Street].

On [September 12, 2005], before the expiration of the agency contract, you [informed this office that the property was no longer available for sale]. Under [Paragraph 6B] of the contract, you agreed to pay [UR Home Realty] [1. 6 percent of the list price 2. the sum of $30,000] if you removed the property from the market [or otherwise made it unmarketable] prior to the expiration of our agreement.

I will be calling you [to arrange a meeting] so we can discuss the reason for your withdrawing your property from the market and to settle any obligations that exist.

Yours truly,

_____

Enclosure: ⟵ *Card*

NOTE: *This letter sets forth the owner's contractual obligation but indicates your desire for an amiable settlement. No threat is being made.*

BUYER BREACH OF PURCHASE AGREEMENT

UR
H O M E   R E A L T Y

_____   ← *Date and*
_____   *address*
_____
_____

Dear _____:

According to your purchase agreement with [Mrs. James Smith] dated [June 1, 2005], for the purchase of [555 Midvale Court], you were required to [increase your deposit by $10,000] no later than [August 3, 2005].

You have failed to meet your contractual obligation. Therefore, I have been authorized as the agent for [Mrs. James Smith] to inform you that your failure is a material breach of your agreement. The seller hereby declares the above contract null and void based on said breach.

[1. Under said agreement, your deposit is to be forfeited as liquidated damages; please sign and return the enclosed forms authorizing the release of your deposit to the sellers as liquidated damages. 2. The sellers reserve the right to bring legal action against you for damages suffered resulting from your breach of contract.]

Yours truly,

_____

Enclosures: ← *Card, release of deposit*

cc: [Mrs. James Smith]

NOTE: *Do not send this letter without specific written authorization from the owners. Always check with your legal representative. Rights vary among states.*

PURCHASE AFTER BUYER AGENCY EXPIRES

UR
H O M E   R E A L T Y

◄—— *Date and address*

Dear _____:

On [September 14, 2005], you entered into an [Exclusive-Authorization-to-Acquire-Property] Agreement with [UR Home Realty]. In accordance with [Paragraph 7B] of this agreement, we provided you with a list of properties we introduced you to. This list, which was given to you on [December 15, 2005], included the [home] owned by [Mr. Morris Black] located at [7314 Elm Ridge Road] in [Middlebury].

On [December 20, 2005], you entered into a contract directly with [Mr. Morris Black] to purchase his [home] for [$600,000]. The sale was completed on [January 15, 2006].

Paragraph [7B.3] of our agreement provides that [UR Home Realty] shall be entitled to our fee if you purchase a property that [we introduced] you to within [90 days] of the expiration of our [Exclusive-Right-to-Acquire-Property] Agreement and we included the property on a list which we provided you [within three days of the expiration of our agreement]. Therefore, in accordance with our agreement, demand is made for the sum of [$18,000].

If you have any questions or desire a meeting, please contact me.

Yours truly,

_____

Enclosure: ◄—— *Card*

NOTE: *A more aggressive approach is called for when buyer and seller get together to cut the agent out of an earned fee. You should consider having your attorney send this letter.*

DEMAND FOR COMMISSION—SALE AFTER LISTING EXPIRES

UR
H O M E   R E A L T Y

_____
_____   ← *Date and*
_____   *address*
_____

Dear _____ :

On [September 14, 2005], which was [ten] days after the expiration of our [Exclusive-Right-to-Sell] listing agreement for your property at [2211 Main Street], you sold said property to [Mr. and Mrs. Jason Lloyd] for the sum of [$740,000]. [No agent was involved in this transaction.]

In accordance with [Paragraph 6A] of the listing agreement, our office provided you the names of [Mr. and Mrs. Jason Lloyd] in writing on [September 4, 2005]. [Our office showed the Main Street property to (Mr. and Mrs. Jason Lloyd) on (August 6 as well as on August 18) and they physically entered the property.]

[Paragraph 6A of the listing] agreement provides that our office is entitled to [our full commission] if a sale is made within [90] days of the expiration of the listing agreement to anyone we showed the property to and whose name we provided to you in writing [within three days of the expiration of the listing agreement].

A sale was made within the designated protection period after the expiration of the listing agreement to a buyer procured by our firm of which you were properly notified in writing. In accordance with [Paragraph 6A.3 of our listing agreement], our office is entitled to the sum of [$44,400]. Demand is hereby made for the remittance of this amount.

Please call me if you have any questions [or would like to arrange a meeting].

Yours truly,

_____

Enclosure: ← *Card*

NOTE: *This is also a case of the buyer and seller getting together to attempt to cut the broker out of his or her fee.*

No threat is made, but the supported facts are laid out. If you have any doubt as to the fact that you were the procuring cause of the subsequent sale, you should check with your attorney. You might want to have this letter sent by your attorney.

NOTICE TO BUILDER OF DEFECT

_____ **UR** _____

H O M E   R E A L T Y

_____ ←— *Date and*
_____   *address*
_____
_____

Dear _____ :

[Mr. and Mrs. Riley], who purchased your [Glenway] home at [8741 Royal Court] through our office, have informed us that [the roof leaks in five places]. They are very concerned about this matter. It would be greatly appreciated if this deficiency were promptly corrected. Small matters often become major problems if not taken care of quickly. More important, an unhappy buyer can detract from both of our reputations.

I look forward to continued beneficial cooperation between our firms and continued success in selling your homes.

Yours truly,

_____

Enclosure: ◄—— *Card*

cc: [Mr. and Mrs. Riley]

NOTE: *This letter sells the benefits of solving the problem and is not threatening. The purpose is to help avoid legal action. It is assumed that the new owner has already made the builder aware of the problem.*

While this is a courtesy letter, should there be legal action, you could be drawn into a lawsuit. Attorneys often will spread a broad net seeking deep pockets when claiming negligence. Therefore, you want to use any clout you have with the builder to resolve the problem. Dissatisfied buyers also have a negative effect on your firm's reputation even if it is not your problem.

OFFICIAL INQUIRY—COMPLAINT

UR
H O M E   R E A L T Y

_____

_____ ◀— *Date and*
                      address
_____

_____

Dear _____:

We have received your letter of [June 3]. I was very surprised that a complaint was made to your office. I have set forth the facts in the attachment and have included signed statements from those in our office who are involved.

Although we believe the complaint is entirely without merit, you can nevertheless expect our full cooperation in this matter. If you have any further questions, please do not hesitate to contact me.

Yours truly,

_____

Enclosures: ◀— *Card, statement of fact, agent statement(s)*

GENERAL COMPLAINT

UR

H O M E   R E A L T Y

◄—— *Date and address*

Dear _____ :

I regret that you have not been satisfied with the [1. services 2. actions] of [UR Home Realty]. Although we don't always succeed, we nevertheless strive in good faith to meet the needs of [both clients and customers]. Our failures are actually important, because they stimulate us to improve.

[1. I will be calling you to arrange a meeting so we can satisfactorily resolve the problem. 2. I want you to know that my door is open to you at any time to discuss problems freely, and I would be happy to meet with you at your convenience.]

Yours truly,

_____

Enclosure: ◄—— *Card*

OFFER TO ARBITRATE / OFFER TO MEET

_____ **UR**

H O M E   R E A L T Y

_____

_____ ← *Date and address*

_____

_____

Dear _____:

[UR Home Realty] would like to resolve [your complaint] in a fair and equitable manner. [What could be fairer than to submit our disagreement to an impartial arbitrator for binding arbitration? If this appears satisfactory to you, please contact me, and we will work out the details of selecting an arbitrator.] [I will call you to arrange a meeting that is convenient to your schedule.]

Yours truly,

_____

Enclosure: ← *Card*

NOTE: *A face-to-face meeting to reach an agreement would generally be preferred to arbitration although arbitration is generally preferable to a lawsuit.*

OFFER TO MEET TO RESOLVE COMPLAINT

UR
H O M E   R E A L T Y

_____   ← *Date and*
_____   *address*
_____
_____

Dear _____:

Based on [1. your letter of July 13   2. our phone conversation on July 13], it is clear that you feel [UR Home Realty] has not treated you in a fair and proper manner.

While I sincerely believe our actions were at all times fair and professional, I am nevertheless disturbed by your feelings toward us. [We consider ourselves a part of the community, and we want very much to maintain a harmonious relationship with all of our neighbors.]

I will contact you in the next few days to arrange a meeting to resolve this problem in a mutually satisfactory manner.

Yours truly,

_____

Enclosure: ◄— *Card*

NOTE: *Whenever possible, settlement offers should be made face-to-face. A meeting is preferable to an offer by letter. It is recommended that an attorney review any settlement offer.*

NOTIFICATION TO STATE DEPARTMENT OF
REAL ESTATE ABOUT VIOLATION OF THE LAW

UR
H O M E   R E A L T Y

⟵ *Date and address*

Dear _____ :

I am sorry to report an apparent violation of our state real estate law by [1. one of my associates 2. a licensed real estate agent].

[On April 12, 2005, Mr. Timothy Jones, a real estate salesperson licensed under my broker's license, accepted a $5,000 cash deposit from Mr. Kermit Pugh. Mr. Jones has not contacted our office since he received the deposit and has not been home in the four days since he accepted the deposit. We therefore assume that Mr. Jones has appropriated the deposit for his own use. We have notified the district attorney of these facts.]

We will fully cooperate with your office in any investigation and will promptly supply any additional information requested.

Yours truly,

_____

Enclosure: ⟵ *Card*

NOTE: *Failure to promptly notify the state licensing authority of a violation of the law could place the broker's license in jeopardy.*

Because of the importance of this letter, consider special handling such as an overnight delivery service that must be signed for upon receipt.

CHAPTER 10

PROPERTY MANAGEMENT

RENTAL INQUIRY

To: _____

From: | agent@urhomerealty.net

Subject: | Available Apartments

Dear _____:

In response to your inquiry, we have the following units available for [1. June 1 occupancy 2. immediate occupancy] that appear to meet your stated requirements:

[Two-bedroom, two-bath at 1822 West Stevens, $1,250/month with $600 security deposit on a one-year lease (no pets).]

[Two-bedroom at 731 West Third Street, $980/month with a $1,000 security deposit on a one-year lease—small pets allowed.]

You can view available apartments on our Web site, [*www.ur-home.net*].

I will be calling you to discuss your real estate needs and to arrange to show you available rental property in [Orchard Ridge]. [We also have several homes and condominiums that can be purchased with very low- and even no-down payment and with monthly payments within your indicated payment range.]

Yours truly,

_____

Attachments: ◀—— *Card, photos*

NOTE: *E-mail with photos would be the preferred method of written communication. If you don't have an e-mail address, consider a phone call to ascertain if the party has access to e-mail messages.*

APPROVAL OF RENTAL APPLICATION

To: _____

From: agent@urhomerealty.net

Subject: Rental Application Approved

Dear _____:

Your rental application has been approved for [733 West Third Street] with occupancy on [November 1].

Please come to [our office] by [October 20] to sign the [one-year] lease and to pay the balance of the required deposits as follows:

[Rent November 1–30]	[$1,150]
[Last month's rent]	[$1,150]
[Security deposit]	[$500]
Total advance rent and deposits	[$2,800]
[Less application deposit]	[($200)]
Balance due:	[$2,600]

I look forward to seeing you.

Yours truly,

_____

Attachment: ◄——— *Card*

NOTE: *An e-mail acceptance would be preferred.*

RENTAL APPLICATION REJECTION #1

To: [   ]

From: [agent@urhomerealty.net   ]

Subject: [Your Rental Application   ]

Dear _____:

I have mailed you [1. your check 2. our check] in the amount of [$175], which constitutes the return of your rental application deposit for [4312 Waverly Way] [less the nonrefundable credit report fee of ($25)].

We have accepted another applicant for the premises.

[We do have several other units available in other buildings:]

Address	Size	Rental
[1732 Third Street	2 BR, 2 Bath	$925]
[501 Chestnut Circle	2 BR, 1 ½ Bath	$875]
[2001 Jupiter Avenue	2 BR, 1 Bath	$790]

[1. If you wish to view any of these units, please contact our office. 2. I will call you in the next few days to arrange to show you any of our offerings that interest you.]

[We also have a number of properties for sale with (1. reasonable 2. low) down payments. If you would like more information on these, please contact me.] The services of [UR Home Realty] are at your disposal to secure suitable housing for your family.

Yours truly,

_____

Attachment: ◄—— *Card*

NOTE: *By mentioning other housing opportunities, and that you will continue to help, you lessen the likelihood that rental applicants will feel discriminated against. Of course, if the reason for rejection of the tenant was poor credit or rental history, you would not want to mention other properties. (See the following letter.)*

Because of the mail delay, a phone call or an e-mail informing the rental applicant of the rejection and that a letter and deposit return have been mailed would be preferable.

RENTAL APPLICATION REJECTION #2

To: _____

From: agent@urhomerealty.net

Subject: Your Rental Application

Dear _____:

We regret to inform you that your rental application for [2001 Jupiter Avenue] has been rejected.

We have mailed you [1. your check 2. our check] for [$300], which represents the return of your rental deposit [less the nonrefundable credit report fee of ($20) as agreed to in your rental application].

If you have any questions, please contact me.

Yours truly,

_____

Attachment: ◀—— *Card*

cc: [Resident property manager]

NOTE: *We strongly suggest that you avoid listing reasons for rejecting applications in your letter, as they tend to lead to protracted confrontations. You should fully document your files, however, because applicants sometimes claim wrongful bias.*

Because of the mail delay, a phone call or an e-mail informing the rental applicant of the rejection and that a letter and deposit return have been mailed would be appropriate.

LATE PAYMENT—WAIVER OF LATE CHARGE

UR

H O M E   R E A L T Y

_____

_____ ◄——— *Date and*
                              address

_____

_____

Dear _____:

Your rent payment for the month of [October 2005] was due at our office no later than [October 10, 2005]. However, we did not receive it until [October 14, 2005].

A late charge of [$50] is authorized by paragraph [six] of your lease.

Because this is your first late payment, we will waive the late charge in this instance. However, it is essential that future rent payments be received on time. If any future rent payment is received late, a late charge will be assessed against you as provided by your lease agreement.

Yours truly,

_____

Enclosure: ◄——— *Card*

cc: [Resident manager]

LATE PAYMENT CHARGE

_____ **UR**
H O M E   R E A L T Y

_____
_____ ◄——— *Date and*
_____   *address*
_____

Dear _____ :

Your rent payment for the month of [October] was due at our office on [October 10]. It was not received until [October 21].

You are hereby notified that in accord with paragraph [four] of your lease, you have been assessed a late charge of [$50].

Please remit this amount immediately.

Yours truly,

_____

Enclosure: ◄——— *Card*

cc: [Resident manager]

BAD CHECK

UR
H O M E   R E A L T Y

_____

_____ ⟵ _Date and_
_____   _address_
_____

Dear _____:

Your check no. [5811] in the amount of [$1,100] made out to [UR Home Realty] for the [April] rent of [Apartment 2700 at 4914 Highland Avenue] has been returned to us from your bank marked insufficient funds.

Please see that this office is furnished with either cash, a money order, cashier's check, or certified check in the amount of [$1,150] by [April 20]. [This amount includes a charge of ($25) for the returned check, under the terms of your lease, as well as a late charge of ($25).] Failure to comply shall be regarded as a breach of your legal obligations.

Yours truly,

_____

Enclosure: ⟵ _Card_

cc: [Resident manager]

NOTE: _No threat of legal action is made, although it might possibly be inferred. A date is set to express urgency. The letter makes clear that a personal check will not be accepted._

Personal delivery of this letter would be preferred but, if mailed, consider registered mail that must be signed for or an overnight delivery service.

RENT INCREASE #1

UR

H O M E   R E A L T Y

_____   ← *Date and*
_____   *address*
_____
_____

Dear _____ :

Because of [1. increased expenses 2. increased interest rates 3. improvements we have made], a rental adjustment has become necessary.

As of [May 1], the rent for [5800 Crescent Cove, #3-S] will be increased from the current [$870] per month to [$910] per month.

Yours truly,

_____

Enclosure: ◄─── *Card*

cc: [Resident property manager]

NOTE: *Be certain that notices comply with your state laws as to content, notice period, and service of the notice (registered mail might be required).*

RENT INCREASE #2

UR

H O M E   R E A L T Y

_____
_____   ◄—— *Date and*
_____   *address*
_____

Dear _____:

You are hereby notified in accord with [Arizona] law that as of [January 1, 2005], your rent shall be increased from [$875] per month to [$925] per month for the premises at [643 Jupiter Lane, second floor].

Yours truly,

_____

Enclosure: ◄—— *Card*

cc: [Resident property manager]

NOTE: *Make certain that rent increase notices are given for the statutory period. For example, a number of states require that notification be given at least 30 days before the rent increase, and in some states the notification period must end on the day rent is due.*

Consider using registered or certified mail, and request return receipts. This avoids the claim of nondelivery or of your notice being mistaken for an advertisement. Your state statutes may specify the manner of delivering the notice as well as the form of the notice.

NOTICE TO CEASE PROHIBITED ACTIVITY /
BREACH OF RULES

UR

H O M E   R E A L T Y

← *Date and address*

Dear _____:

It has come to our attention that [you have been performing major automobile repair work in your parking space at 110 Stardust Lane].

This is a violation of [1. your lease 2. the occupancy rules and regulations you signed at the time of rental].

You are hereby ordered to cease this activity immediately, or corrective action shall be required in accord with your lease.

Yours truly,

_____

Enclosure: ◄— *Card*

cc: [Resident property manager]

E-MAIL TO RESIDENT MANAGER—PROBLEMS

To: [_____]

From: [agent@urhomerealty.net]

Subject: [Property Deficiencies]

Dear _____:

[1. An inspection of the property at (1295 Plymouth Circle) revealed the following (1. deficiency 2. deficiencies): 2. We have received a complaint regarding the following:]

- [Sprinklers are spraying into the street.]
- [The garbage container is often left open, which attracts flies.]
- [Three of the exterior lights are inoperative.]

Please rectify the [1. problem(s) 2. deficiency 3. deficiencies] [1. as soon as practical 2. immediately] and notify me as to the action taken.

If you have any questions, please contact me.

Yours truly,

_____

Attachment: ◀—— *Card*

NOTE: *Phone, e-mail, or fax notification would be preferable to a letter because of letter delays.*

NOTICE TO TENANT—
FAILURE TO MAINTAIN EXTERIOR OR LAWN

UR
H O M E   R E A L T Y

_____
_____   ←— _Date and_
_____   _address_
_____

Dear _____:

In [1. driving by 2. inspecting] the [home at 12 West Davis Street], which you are renting from our office, I was surprised to see that [the lawn has not been cared for].

Under the terms of your lease, you are required to [maintain the landscaping]. Unless [the lawn is properly maintained by August 1], we shall have to contract for the work with [a gardening service] and add the charges to your rent.

Yours truly,

_____

Enclosure: ◄—— _Card_

NOTICE OF LEASE AUTOMATIC RENEWAL

UR
H O M E   R E A L T Y

_____
_____   ◄——— *Date and*
                          address
_____
_____

Dear _____:

Your present lease for [the two-bedroom house] at [660 Stardust Circle]
expires on [January 1, 2006].

This is to remind you that unless you give notice to the contrary by
[December 1, 2005], the lease by its terms will be automatically extended for
[another year]. If you have any questions, please contact me.

Yours truly,

_____

Enclosure: ◄——— *Card*

cc: [Resident property manager]

NOTE: *Although many owners don't remind tenants of the automatic renewal, the reminder does avoid future problems. In some states, automatic renewal cannot be enforced.*

LEASE EXPIRATION NOTICE—NEW LEASE

UR
H O M E   R E A L T Y

——————————— ← *Date and*
———————————   *address*
———————————
———————————

Dear ————————————:

Your lease for [660 Maple Lane] expires on [September 1, 2005]. I have enclosed a new lease for the premises substantially the same as your old lease [1. at the same rent   2. except that the rent has been increased to ($1,400). The higher rent is required because of cost increases in the operation and management of the property].

Please sign and return [two] copies of the new lease to my office by [July 15, 2005]. If I do not receive your new lease by this date, I will assume that you do not wish to remain in possession and we shall seek a new tenant.

Yours truly,

————————————

Enclosures: ← *Card, lease*

cc: [Resident apartment manager]

NOTE: *Although it is not necessary to give reasons for a rent increase, a reason makes your action seem less arbitrary and helps to maintain better tenant relations.*
Rather than mailing the letter and lease, a better approach would be for the apartment manager to hand-deliver it to the tenant.

TENANT NOTICE OF LEAVING IN VIOLATION OF LEASE

UR
H O M E   R E A L T Y

—————————
————————— ◄—— *Date and*
—————————   *address*
—————————

Dear _____ :

Your current lease, dated [January 1, 2005], does not expire until [January 1, 2006]. If you wish to vacate the premises before this date, you will be held liable for the cost of re-renting the premises as well as any rental loss incurred.

If you wish to locate a tenant to assume your lease obligations, we will allow a lease assignment subject to our approval based on our reasonable rental criteria. You, of course, would remain liable if the new tenant defaults on the lease.

Please contact me immediately about your intentions. If you are vacating on [September 1, as you indicated], I want to begin immediately to find a new tenant in order to keep your legal obligations to a minimum.

Yours truly,

_____

Enclosure: ◄—— *Card*

cc: [Resident apartment manager]

NOTE: *This notice should be sent by registered mail or an overnight delivery service to emphasize its importance.*

TENANT VACATED IN VIOLATION OF LEASE

UR
H O M E   R E A L T Y

_____   ← *Date and*
_____   *address*
_____
_____

Dear _____:

I have been informed that on [April 15] you vacated the premises at
[1700 Sycamore Avenue]. [1. Your lease required a 30-day notice, which was
not given. 2. Your lease does not expire until (June 1).] Therefore, you shall be
held liable [1. for the rental until the end of the lease period   2. for the 30-day
notice period expiring (May 15)].

If we are able to re-rent the premises prior to the above date, your liability
will be reduced by the rent received for said period less the costs of re-renting
the premises.

Please contact this office immediately to make arrangements for fulfilling
your obligation.

Yours truly,

_____

Enclosure: ← *Card*

cc: [Resident apartment manager]

NOTE: *This letter might require modification based on state law. Contact legal counsel.*

NOTICE TO VACATE

_____

UR

H O M E   R E A L T Y

_____

_____   ← *Date and*
_____   *address*
_____
_____

Dear _____ :

In accord with [1. the terms of your tenancy 2. (Arizona) law], you are hereby notified that you are ordered to vacate the premises at [6603 Sycamore Parkway] by [May 1, 2005]. This notice shall constitute the [30-day notice] required by [state law].

Agent for: [UR Home Management]

_____

Enclosure: ← *Card*

cc: [Resident manager]

NOTE: *Be certain that your notice and the service of the notice conform with your state law (legal forms can be used in lieu of a letter). Registered mail or personal service might be required. You may have to post the notice on the door to the premises. In some states, the notification period must end on the day rent is due. Check with an attorney, and then modify the notice if required.*

ACKNOWLEDGMENT OF TENANT'S NOTICE TO VACATE

UR
H O M E   R E A L T Y

_____
_____   ◄——— *Date and*
_____   *address*
_____

Dear _____:

We acknowledge your notice to vacate the premises at [3120 West Lincoln, Unit 8] by [March 1, 2006].

You will be called by [1. the manager, (Mr. Jones), 2. this office] to arrange to show your [apartment] to prospective renters. We will try to give you as much notice as possible.

[Mr. Jones], the [Resident Manager], will conduct an inspection of the unit when you have vacated. After the inspection, your property damage bond will be returned to you less any rent that may be due and damage [or missing property] other than normal wear and tear.

If you have any questions or desire help in locating housing, please contact us.

Yours truly,

_____

Enclosure: ◄——— *Card*

cc: [Resident property manager]

TENANT LETTER—END-OF-LEASE INSPECTION

UR

H O M E   R E A L T Y

Date and ← *address*

Dear _____:

In accord with [1. your notice 2. our notice 3. the rental agreement], you will be vacating the premises at [1140 Hercules Court, Unit 8B] on [April 30].

We will be conducting an inspection of the premises at [2:00 P.M.], [April 30], to determine whether there is any damage to the premises other than normal wear and tear [and whether any items are missing from the premises]. [1. After this inspection 2. Within (60) days of this inspection], your security deposit will be returned to you minus deductions for any damage to the premises [or for any missing items].

If you wish, you may be present for this inspection.

Yours truly,

_____

Enclosure: ← *Card*

cc: [Resident manager]

NOTE: *This letter reminds tenants that they should leave the premises in good condition, and it will probably reduce the cleaning requirements prior to re-renting.*

NOTICE TO TENANT OF DAMAGE ON VACATING PREMISES

UR

H O M E   R E A L T Y

_____   _Date and_
                ◄——— _address_
_____

_____

_____

Dear _____:

Inspection of the premises at [6603 Sycamore, third floor] that you vacated on [April 1] revealed that [1. the living room floor is badly scratched in several places 2. the ceiling fan and miniblinds from the dining room are missing 3. the bathroom mirror is broken].

Because the [1. damages 2. missing articles] are not normal wear and tear, we have made the necessary [1. repairs 2. replacements] and have deducted the cost, [$325], from your [security deposit]. [The balance of ($75) is enclosed.]

[Because the cost of (1. repairs 2. replacements), ($500), exceeds the amount of your property damage bond, please remit ($300) to this office no later than (4 P.M.) on (April 10).]

[The necessary (1. repairs 2. replacements) have resulted in costs of ($300). Please remit this amount to our office no later than (4 P.M.) on (April 10).]

Yours truly,

_____

Enclosures: ◄——— _Card, property damage bond statement_

cc: [Resident manager]

NOTE: _By using a definite date for the alternative paragraphs, the former tenant will assume that legal action will be taken if the remittance is not paid by this date, although no threat is being made._
    An overnight delivery service should be considered for this letter.

TENANT COMPLAINT—FORWARDED FOR ACTION

To:	
From:	agent@urhomerealty.net
Subject:	Problem to Be Resolved Soon

Dear _____:

I have received your [letter] about [the unauthorized parking in your space].

I have forwarded your concerns to [the resident manager] who will be contacting you directly.

I sincerely hope that the problem is resolved to your satisfaction. If you have any other questions, call the manager or me.

Yours truly,

_____

cc: [Resident manager]

NOTE: *If an e-mail address was given or the complaint was received by e-mail, this response should be by e-mail.*

TENANT COMPLAINT—ACTION TAKEN

To: [   ]

From: [agent@urhomerealty.net   ]

Subject: [Problem Resolved   ]

Dear _____:

I have received your [letter] about [unauthorized parking in your space].

[The offending party has been contacted], and we hope that the [problem has been resolved]. If the problem continues, please contact [1. me directly 2. (Mr. Brown), the building manager].

Yours truly,

_____

Attachment: ◄─── *Card*

cc: [Mr. Brown]

NOTE: *If an e-mail address was given or the complaint was received by e-mail, this response should be by e-mail.*

TENANT COMPLAINT—NO ACTION TAKEN

UR

H O M E   R E A L T Y

_____

_____   ⟵— _Date and_
                                 address
_____

_____

Dear _____ :

I have received your complaint [that the neighbor's children have been disturbing you]. [Because we do not discriminate as to families, the noise of children playing must be expected, although it can be exasperating at times.]

[1. Because we are unable to solve your problem, we would be willing to allow you to break your lease upon (30) days' notice. Please let me know what you decide.   2. When your lease expires, we would be happy to help you find a unit that better meets your requirements.]

Yours truly,

_____

Enclosure: ⟵— _Card_

cc: [Resident manager]

NOTICE TO TENANT OF LESSOR ENTRY

UR
H O M E   R E A L T Y

_____

_____   ← _Date and address_

_____

_____

Dear _____ :

In accord with the terms of our lease, we will be [1. making an inspection of the premises 2. showing the premises to a prospective buyer 3. repairing the kitchen floor in your unit] at [9 A.M.] on [Tuesday, February 6].

If you are unable to be there at that time, please contact [1. this office 2. Mr. Brown, the Building Manager] [1. so a more convenient time can be arranged 2. to make certain that the building manager has all necessary keys].

Yours truly,

_____

Enclosure: ← _Card_

cc: [Building manager]

NOTE: _A phone call would be the preferable way to inform the tenant._

NOTICE OF WORK ON PREMISES

UR

H O M E   R E A L T Y

_____ ←—— *Date and*
_____   *address*
_____
_____

Dear _____:

In the next [1. few days 2. few weeks], we will be [1. painting the lobby
2. replacing the air conditioning]. We hope that you will not be inconvenienced
by the work, which will be confined to normal working hours.

[Access to your apartment will be required on (April 15). If you are not home,
our resident manager, (Jane Smith), will remain in your unit while workers are
present. (Please provide keys to the manager if required.)]

Yours truly,

_____

Enclosure: ←—— *Card*

cc: [Resident manager]

NOTE: *This letter serves another purpose, in that it informs the tenants they
are getting something for their rent; the owner is putting money back into the
building. This service makes a subsequent rent increase more palatable to the
tenants.*

CONFIRMATION OF TELEPHONE WORK ORDER

UR

H O M E   R E A L T Y

_____
_____   ← _Date and_
                    address
_____
_____

Dear _____:

This will confirm our agreement on [May 10] for you to [provide a pest control inspection] at [6501 Crescent Circle]. It is understood that the work must be completed by [June 1].

[Please call our office 24 hours before you begin work so we can be certain someone will be present to provide access to the property.]

We acknowledge that your charge for said work shall be [$125].

[Work order number (1073) has been assigned to this project. Please reference said work order in any billing or other correspondence.]

[Bill (1. this office 2. Mr. and Mrs. James) for the work no later than (July 1).]

Yours truly,

_____

Enclosure: ◄── _Card_

cc: [Resident manager]

REPAIR REQUEST TO OWNER—AUTHORIZATION REQUIRED

_____ **UR** _____

H O M E   R E A L T Y

_____
_____ ← _Date and address_
_____
_____

Dear _____ :

Your property at [74181 Lexington Avenue] requires the following repairs:

- [Exterior lighting needs to be replaced to comply with code requirements.]
- [Replacement of condensor unit for Apartment 2C air conditioner.]

Based on the enclosed [1. estimate 2. bid], [1. the cost for this work will be ($1,470) 2. the cost for this work is likely to exceed ($1,000)].

Our management contract requires your authorization for any repair that exceeds [$1,000]. We therefore request your authorization to make the required repairs. Failure to authorize repairs could result in [1. vacancies and loss of income 2. damage to the property 3. being cited for code violations].

Your prompt attention to this matter would be appreciated.

Yours truly,

_____

Enclosures: ← _Card, bid, photos_

cc: [Resident Manager]

NOTE: _If a photo of the problem would help to indicate the necessity of the work, enclosing a photo should be considered._

BROKER, LENDER, AND ATTORNEY LETTERS

WELCOME TO NEW BROKER

UR

H O M E   R E A L T Y

_____
_____ ← *Date and*
_____   *address*
_____

Dear _____:

As a fellow [1. real estate broker 2. REALTOR®] I would like to welcome you
to [the growing West Side].

I am certain that we will have many productive dealings in the coming years
because cooperation is the basis of real estate success. I will stop by to meet
you personally in a few weeks after you are settled.

I wish you success in your new office—welcome!

Sincerely,

_____

Enclosure: ←— *Card*

E-MAIL MLS CARAVAN—BREAKFAST OR LUNCH

To:	
From:	agent@urhomerealty.net
Subject:	CARAVAN—[October 28] [Buffet]

Be sure to visit [37 West Toliver Avenue] and be my guest for a

[1. **Continental Breakfast**
2. **Breakfast Buffet**
3. **Very Special Brunch**
4. **Luncheon Buffet**]

from [9 A.M.–11 A.M.]

_____ [UR Home Realty]

NOTE: *In areas where there are more listings than agents can possibly visit, you may need something extra to bring in agents. Food will act as a magnet in these situations. While letters could be used, you could send an e-mail. By clicking on the address, the recipient could view photos or a virtual tour, and property details.*

E-MAIL INVITATION—AGENT OPEN HOUSE

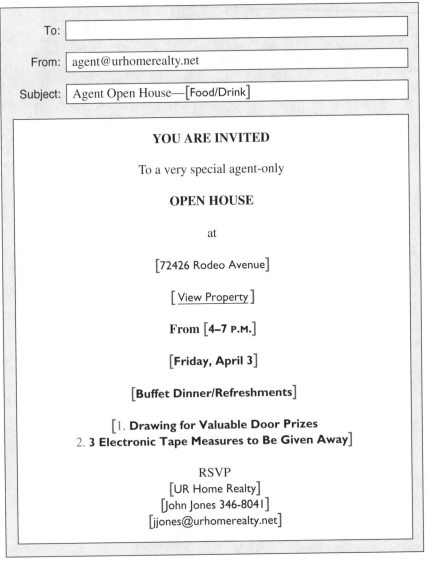

To:

From: agent@urhomerealty.net

Subject: Agent Open House—[Food/Drink]

YOU ARE INVITED

To a very special agent-only

OPEN HOUSE

at

[72426 Rodeo Avenue]

[View Property]

From [4–7 P.M.]

[Friday, April 3]

[Buffet Dinner/Refreshments]

[1. **Drawing for Valuable Door Prizes**
2. **3 Electronic Tape Measures to Be Given Away**]

RSVP
[UR Home Realty]
[John Jones 346-8041]
[jjones@urhomerealty.net]

NOTE: *An RSVP will usually increase attendance because it makes the invitation more special to the recipients, and once they have responded, they are more likely to actually come.*

OFFICE OPEN HOUSE INVITATION

[UR Home Realty]

Open House

[922 West Broadway]

[Wednesday, April 5]

[5–8 P.M.]

Come visit with us at our [1. new office   2. new branch office].

Refreshments will be served!

NOTE: *This invitation could be sent to owners, investors, escrow and title companies, and lenders, as well as other brokers and salespeople. We suggest that you have this invitation printed on regular invitation stock.*

HOLIDAY OPEN HOUSE INVITATION

[UR Home Realty]

Cordially Invites You to Our Holiday Season Open House

[922 West 52nd Street]

[Friday December 23]

[5–7 P.M.]

Please Visit with Us

Refreshments will be served.

[Sprig of holly here]

NOTE: *Invitations should be on regular invitation card stock. Send to other brokers, lenders, investors, owners, and so on.*

BROKER REFERRAL THANK YOU

UR
H O M E   R E A L T Y

_____
←— *Date and*
_____   *address*
_____
_____

Dear _____:

Thank you very much for referring [Jane Smith] to this office.

I have shown [the Smiths] a number of properties [and I am confident I will be able to meet their housing needs].

[I hope I will be sending you a check within a short time.]

If I can ever be of service to you, don't hesitate to call me.

Yours truly,

_____

Enclosure: ←— *Card*

BROKER REFERRAL THANK YOU—NO SALE

UR
H O M E   R E A L T Y

_____
             ←___ *Date and*
_____   *address*

_____

_____

Dear _____:

Thank you very much for referring [Joseph Jones] to our office. Although we contacted [the Joneses] promptly [and showed them a number of homes], we regret that we were unsuccessful in providing for their home purchase.

I want you to know that our failure was not the result of lack of effort. In fact, if there is another opportunity, I would like to show you that [UR Home Realty] does make sales and is worthy of your referrals.

Yours truly,

_____

Enclosure: ←___ *Card*

BROKER REFERRAL—NOTICE OF SALE

UR
H O M E   R E A L T Y

———————————
← *Date and*
———————————   *address*
———————————
———————————

Dear _____:

Just a note to let you know that [Sylvia Smith], whom you referred to us, has [purchased a home through this office]. The closing is scheduled for [June 1]. On closing, we will immediately forward your referral fee of [$4,802] based on our office commission of [$24,010].

We appreciate the referral and look forward to future cooperation with your office.

Yours truly,

———————————

Enclosure: ←— *Card*

REFERRAL FEE—TRANSMITTAL

UR

H O M E   R E A L T Y

Date and
address ←

Dear _____ :

Enclosed is our check in the amount of [$4,802] for your referral of [John Jones] as well as our commission statement. Thank you again for recommending [UR Home Realty].

We look forward to working with you in the future.

Yours truly,

_____

Enclosures: ←— _Card, check, commission statement_

SEEKING AN INVESTMENT PROPERTY

UR

H O M E   R E A L T Y

_____ ← *Date and*
_____   *address*
_____
_____

Dear _____:

I am working with a prospective investor who has [more than $500,000] to invest and desires [1. residential property 2. commercial property 3. a raw-land investment]. My buyer's primary objective is [1. appreciation 2. income 3. tax-sheltered income]. [Safety is, of course, a consideration as well.]

My investor [1. wants a positive cash flow 2. will accept a negative cash flow 3. wants at least a break-even cash flow] with an [1. all-cash 2. moderately leveraged 3. highly leveraged] investment.

If you have any investment property listed with your office that you believe would interest my buyer, I would very much like to work with you.

Yours truly,

_____

Enclosure: ◄— *Card*

REQUEST FOR COMMISSION

UR
H O M E   R E A L T Y

⟵ *Date and address*

Dear _____ :

[On the morning of October 12, Mrs. Jean Jacobs of our office showed a home that you have listed at 1112 Kings Drive to Mr. and Mrs. William Apple. That afternoon, you held an Open House at the same property, and Mr. and Mrs. William Apple stopped at the house. They have indicated that they told your salesperson, Jim Peters, that they had seen the house that morning with Mrs. Jacobs. Mr. Peters proceeded to prepare a purchase agreement, which the Apples signed and the owner accepted.] These facts clearly indicate that [UR Home Realty] was the procuring cause for the sale and is therefore entitled to the sales commission.

I will be calling you to arrange a meeting so this matter can be resolved.

Yours truly,

_____

Enclosure: ⟵ *Card*

NOTE: *An attempt to resolve a problem such as this should preferably be made in person or by phone.*

BROKER COMMISSION SPLIT—TRANSMITTAL

UR
H O M E   R E A L T Y

_____
_____ ⟵ *Date and*
_____   *address*
_____

Dear _____:

Enclosed is our check for [$11,850], which represents [50] percent of the total commission for [your sale] of the property located at [5 Sycamore Circle] to [Janet Smith].

I have enclosed a copy of the closing statement for your records.

Your cooperation was greatly appreciated, and I look forward to sending you many more commissions.

Yours truly,

_____

Enclosures: ⟵ *Card, check, closing statement*

BREACH OF PROCEDURE BY OUR OFFICE

UR
H O M E   R E A L T Y

⟵ *Date and address*

Dear _____:

I want to apologize personally to you for an unfortunate breach of proce-
dure by our office. [1. On June 16, one of our salespeople contacted one of
your owners, Janet Smith, without going through your office. 2. One of our
salespeople contacted James Smith, whose listing was in full effect with your
office, about obtaining a listing.] The reasons for the breach and the fact that
at the time the salesperson did not realize that [1. he 2. she] was in breach
of ethics does not matter.

What does matter is that one of my salespeople failed to respect your rights.
I have already discussed the situation with my salesperson. Rest assured that
I will do everything in my power to make certain that such an action is not
repeated.

Yours truly,

_____

Enclosure: ⟵ *Card*

BREACH OF PROCEDURE BY YOUR OFFICE

UR

H O M E   R E A L T Y

_____
←— *Date and*
_____   *address*

_____

_____

Dear _____:

I am sorry to have to inform you that on [August 21] your salesperson, [Sylvia Smith], [contacted James Smith, whose listing was in full effect with our office, about obtaining a listing].

This type of action cannot be condoned because, in our profession, cooperation is the basis of success. We hope that such action is not repeated in the future.

Yours truly,

_____

Enclosure: ◄— *Card*

ARBITRATION NOTICE

UR
H O M E   R E A L T Y

_____
⟵ *Date and*
_____   *address*
_____
_____

Dear _____ :

Based on your failure to pay [UR Home Realty the selling commission for the sale of 1112 Kings Drive to Mr. and Mrs. William Apple], we are requesting arbitration [of this matter with the San Marco Board of REALTORS® in accord with board rules and regulations].

Yours truly,

_____

Enclosure: ⟵ *Card*

NOTE: *Mandatory arbitration is possible when both parties are members of an organization that requires arbitration.*

LOAN APPLICATION TRANSMITTAL

UR
H O M E   R E A L T Y

_____   ← *Date and*
_____   *address*
_____
_____

Dear _____:

Enclosed you will find the completed loan application of [John and Mary Brown] for the purchase of a home located at [65 Jupiter Lane].

If you have any problems whatsoever or desire any additional information, please contact me [or Meg Smith].

Yours truly,

_____

Enclosures: ← *Card, loan application*

cc: [John and Mary Brown]

NOTE: *We suggest sending loan package overnight delivery such as FedEx when it cannot be delivered in person or an e-mail application is not possible.*

REQUEST TO LENDER TO EXPEDITE LOAN REQUEST

UR
H O M E   R E A L T Y

_____ ← *Date and*
_____   *address*
_____
_____

Dear _____ :

[Mr. and Mrs. Smith] recently applied for a loan through your office for the purchase of the home at [111 Stardust Circle].

Because of unusual needs of the [1. seller 2. buyer], it is necessary that this sale be closed by [August 1, 2005]. Although I realize that this places a strain on your office, I would nevertheless greatly appreciate any efforts you can provide to expedite this transaction.

Yours truly,

_____

Enclosure: ← *Card*

cc: [Mr. and Mrs. Smith]

NOTE: *A better approach would be a phone call to the loan officer and phone or e-mail monitoring of the status of the loan.*

TO LENDER—LOW APPRAISAL

To: _____

From: agent@urhomerealty.net

Subject: RE: Appraisal for [1121 Hummingbird Circle]

Dear _____:

I was surprised by the appraisal made on [April 3] for the property at [1121 Hummingbird Circle] for [Mr. and Mrs. Jones's] loan application.

The appraisal of [$260,000] does not appear to reflect recent sales of comparable property in the area.

I have attached a comparative market analysis based on all the sales in [the Orchard Ridge subdivision] within the past [90 days]. You will see from comparable sales that your appraisal, as stated, appears to be at least [$60,000] under current market value.

I would appreciate the appraisal being reviewed.

I have enjoyed our mutually beneficial relationship in the past, and hope to continue working with you in the future to arrange the financing for our real estate purchasers.

Yours truly,

_____

Attachment: ◄— *Comparative market analysis*

cc: [1. Buyer 2. Seller]

NOTE: *Consider a phone call to the loan officer and e-mail of the letter and enclosure.*

REQUEST FOR ABSTRACT UPDATE

UR

H O M E   R E A L T Y

_____

_____   ←——— *Date and*
                                  address

_____

_____

Dear _____:

Please update the enclosed abstract for the following described property:
[insert legal description of property].

Please bill [the seller, Thomas Pike,] for this service.

Yours truly,

_____

Enclosures: ←——— *Card, abstract*

cc: [Names of buyer and/or seller]

NOTE: *The abstract should normally be delivered personally. If it is mailed or sent by messenger, obtain a receipt as proof of its delivery.*

If an escrow agent is used, the escrow agent will handle updating of the abstract.

THANK YOU TO LOAN OFFICER #1

UR

HOME REALTY

_____

_____   ← *Date and*

_____   *address*

_____

Dear _____ :

I would like to personally thank you for your help in arranging the financing for [Sherman and Joyce Mack] for their recent purchase of the home at [72 Lynn Court].

You not only delivered the loan in a timely manner, but you provided counseling service as well, which was greatly appreciated. You turned what is usually a difficult process for a buyer into a pleasant experience. I hope to work with you and your firm on many future loans.

Yours truly,

_____

Enclosure: ← *Card*

cc: [Jane Smith, President, ABO Savings Association]

NOTE: *A letter such as this, with copies sent to the president of the lender or loan broker, will be appreciated by the loan officer. You can expect this loan officer to treat any future loan problems as a priority item.*

THANK YOU TO LOAN OFFICER #2

UR
H O M E   R E A L T Y

_____
_____ ◄—— *Date and*
_____   *address*
_____

Dear _____ :

I want to thank you personally for your Herculean efforts that resulted in our closing the [James C. Smith] loan by [August 1].

Your attention to detail and your honest, straightforward approach proved that what others said couldn't be done can be accomplished with a positive, "can do" attitude. Working with you was a pleasure, and I look forward to many further transactions with your firm.

Yours truly,

_____

Enclosure: ◄—— *Card*

cc: [John Jones, President, ABC Savings Association]

NOTE: *This letter and its copy will give you a future ally in the lender's office.*

REQUEST FOR LIST OF REOs

UR
H O M E   R E A L T Y

_____
_____ ◄——— *Date and*
_____   *address*
_____

Dear _____:

Please provide a list of your present repossessions and give the following information:

1. Address and size

2. Price and terms (if applicable)

3. Obtaining keys for showings (Is a master key available?)

Yours truly,

_____

Enclosure: ◄——— *Card*

NOTE: *REO is the trade acronym for real estate owned by the lender that is acquired through foreclosure.*

REQUEST FOR ATTORNEY TITLE OPINION

UR
HOME REALTY

_____ ← *Date and*
_____   *address*
_____
_____

Dear _____:

Please provide a title opinion for [Mr. and Mrs. Thomas Wooley] for the purchase of [legal description of property].

The updated abstract is enclosed.

Please send the opinion and the abstract to [my office]. Your invoice should be made out to [Mr. and Mrs. Thomas Wooley, but sent to me].

Yours truly,

_____

Enclosures: ← *Card, abstract*

cc: [Mr. and Mrs. Thomas Wooley]

NOTE: *Generally, abstracts should be hand-delivered to the attorney's office and a receipt should be obtained. In most of the country, title opinions have been replaced by title insurance.*

PURCHASE CONTRACT FOR BUYER'S/SELLER'S ATTORNEY APPROVAL

UR
HOME REALTY

_____   ← *Date and*
_____   *address*
_____
_____

Dear _____:

Enclosed is the completed purchase contract for the [1. sale by 2. purchase by] [Jim and Jane Schmidt] of [111 Crescent Cove]. If, after your review, you determine that the agreement is legally sufficient, please have [Mr. and Mrs. Schmidt] sign and return [three] copies to this office.

Yours truly,

_____

Enclosures: ←— *Card, purchase contract*

cc: [Jim and Jane Schmidt]

NOTE: *Don't mention changes or modifications. Most attorneys will do so without your reminder.*

THANK-YOU LETTER TO ATTORNEY

UR
H O M E   R E A L T Y

_____
_____   ◄—— *Date and*
_____   *address*
_____

Dear _____ :

Working with you on the [Smiths'] [1. sale 2. purchase] was a pleasure. Your professional and helpful manner made what can sometimes be confrontational a friendly and beneficial transaction.

If I am ever asked to recommend a real estate attorney, I will not hesitate to provide your name.

Yours truly,

_____

Enclosure: ◄—— *Card*

NOTE: *A thank-you letter such as this will help you to deal with the attorney in a more relaxed manner in the future.*

REQUEST FOR ESCROW FEE AND COST SCHEDULES

UR
H O M E   R E A L T Y

_____   ← *Date and*
_____   *address*
_____
_____

Dear _____:

Please supply me with your current escrow fee schedule as well as your schedule of escrow costs.

Thanking you in advance,

_____

Enclosure: ◄— *Card*

REQUEST FOR PRIVATE MORTGAGE
INSURANCE INFORMATION

UR
H O M E   R E A L T Y

⟵ *Date and*
  address

Dear _____ :

Please send me information on your requirements for and costs of private mortgage insurance. Please also include several application packages.

I am looking forward to receiving the material and I hope it will lead to a mutually beneficial relationship.

Yours truly,

_____

Enclosure: ⟵ *Card*

INQUIRY ABOUT HOME PROTECTION WARRANTY

UR
H O M E   R E A L T Y

_____

_____ ← *Date and*
                    address

_____

_____

Dear _____ :

Please send me information, costs, and coverage for your home warranty programs as well as several application packages.

I am looking forward to receiving the material and I hope it will lead to a mutually beneficial relationship.

Yours truly,

_____

Enclosure: ◄— *Card*

INQUIRY ABOUT ESCROW STATUS FOR CLOSING

To: _____

From: agent@urhomerealty.net

Subject: Escrow Status

Dear _____:

Please provide me with the present status of the escrow for closing on [111 West Jackson Street], [Hirt—sellers, and Scallon—buyers].

If there is any problem that could prevent a [June 1] closing, please contact me at once. Thank you.

Yours truly,

_____

Attachment: ◄— *Card*

cc: [J. Hirt and L. Scallon]

NOTE: *An e-mail or phone message would be preferable to a letter because it provides an immediate inquiry.*

ORDER TO RETURN OR TURN OVER DEPOSIT

UR

H O M E   R E A L T Y

Date and ←
address

To: [1. Escrow agent 2. Attorney holding a deposit]

Dear _____:

You are holding an earnest money deposit for [$10,000], pursuant to a [purchase agreement] dated [October 1, 2005], in which [Mr. and Mrs. Joseph Scallon] agreed to buy [the home at 6116 Elm Street West] from [Mrs. John Dooley]. [Enclosed is a release authorization signed by (the Scallons and Mrs. Dooley).]

You are hereby authorized to [1. return 2. turn over] [1. the deposit 2. the sum of ($10,000)] to [1. Mr. and Mrs. Joseph Scallon 2. Mrs. John Dooley].

Yours truly,

_____

Enclosures: ← *Card, copy of buyer/seller authorization to return or turn over deposit*

cc: [Mr. and Mrs. Joseph Scallon, Mrs. John Dooley]

NOTE: *This is an order to a third-party escrow holder about return of deposit money when the sale will not be completed. The sellers must agree to the return of the deposit to the buyers, or the buyers must agree to turn over their deposit to the seller.*

12

PERSONNEL LETTERS

REAL ESTATE CAREER NIGHT ANNOUNCEMENT

Join Us for Real Estate Career Night

- Learn how many people have found new direction in their lives through real estate.

- Learn the following benefits that a professional career in real estate offers:

  ✓ The personal satisfaction of helping others

  ✓ The independence of planning your own work

  ✓ Financial rewards directly related to your success in helping meet housing needs

  ✓ Constant mental stimulation in facing unique challenges

If you are a retiree, a homemaker re-entering the work force, a recent graduate, or are simply interested in a career change, this is your opportunity to learn how a real estate career can meet your needs and to ask any questions you might have.

[Thursday, April 8]

[7:00 P.M.]

[UR Home Realty]

[473 N. Main]

[RSVP] [555-8200]

NOTE: *This notice can be mailed on invitation stock as an invitation or mailed as a letter. It can also be used as a flyer. Good places to leave or post flyers are senior centers and condominium association clubhouses.*

**NEW OR PROSPECTIVE
REAL ESTATE SALESPERSON SOLICITATION**

UR

H O M E   R E A L T Y

_____ ⟵ *Date and*
_____   *address*

_____

_____

Dear _____ :

I understand you [1. are currently enrolled in a real estate license preparatory course 2. have applied to take your real estate salesperson's examination 3. have recently passed your real estate salesperson's examination]. I wish you success, and I hope you find a career in real estate is as personally rewarding for you as it has been for many of us.

[UR Home Realty] is looking for people who are sincerely seeking a career, not just a job. People who want professional growth so they can meet the needs of others. People with integrity and motivation. These are the kinds of individuals who can be successful real estate salespersons.

If you feel your goals are compatible with ours, and you have not made a decision as to broker affiliation, call me so we can arrange to meet to discuss a possible career with [UR Home Realty]. We want you to learn about us as we learn about you.

Sincerely,

_____

Enclosure: ⟵ *Card*

NOTE: *Some states sell lists of names of applicants for licensing examinations, as well as lists of names of those who passed their examinations. Some license preparatory schools will also provide names of students.*

SALESPERSON SOLICITATION—RETIRED

UR
H O M E   R E A L T Y

_____   ← *Date and*
_____   *address*
_____
_____

Dear _____:

Are you

Tired of Being Retired?

If you like people, have good character, and are not afraid to start a new career, I would like to meet with you.

I can offer you the personal satisfaction of helping others, a feeling of self-worth working in an independent environment, mental stimulation, and financial rewards earned by your success. After a short license-training program, we will work with you and guide you in your career.

Interested? Then call me today so we can meet to discuss a career in real estate.

Yours truly,

_____

Enclosure: ◄— *Card*

NOTE: *This letter can be mailed to people living in retirement-oriented developments or modified for use as a flyer and distributed in retirement communities as well as in senior centers.*

WELCOME NEW AGENT (LARGE OR MULTIOFFICE BROKER)

UR
HOME REALTY

Date and address ←

_____
_____
_____
_____

Dear _____:

Welcome to [UR Home Realty]!

Our goal at [UR Home Realty] is to serve the needs of buyers and sellers to the best of our abilities. To accomplish this goal, we must be knowledgeable professionals. Therefore, we encourage your professional growth, and we will do all we can to guide you in your success.

I look forward to a long and mutually beneficial association. If any problems arise or if we can provide any assistance, please let us know.

Sincerely,

_____

Enclosure: ← *Card*

NOTE: *In all but the largest offices, the broker should meet personally with the new salesperson.*

TRAINING SESSION NOTICE

UR

H O M E   R E A L T Y

MEMO

Attention All Sale Personnel!

Training Session:
[Wednesday, April 1, 9 A.M.–10 A.M. (Prior to Caravan)]

Subject:
[Listing Techniques]

[If you are unable to attend, please contact (Jane Jones) as soon as possible.]

[Coffee and rolls will be served.]

NOTE: *If the firm has multiple offices, include the location of the session.*
If salespersons do not pick up messages at the office, this memo should be in the form of an e-mail.

SALES MEETING NOTICE

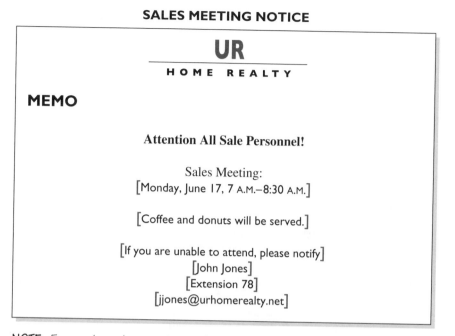

UR

H O M E   R E A L T Y

MEMO

Attention All Sale Personnel!

Sales Meeting:
[Monday, June 17, 7 A.M.–8:30 A.M.]

[Coffee and donuts will be served.]

[If you are unable to attend, please notify]
[John Jones]
[Extension 78]
[jjones@urhomerealty.net]

NOTE: *For regular sales meetings, a form can be used with the date inserted. If the firm has multiple offices, include the location of the meeting.*

If salespersons do not pick up messages at the office, this memo should be in the form of an e-mail.

NOTICE TO SALESPERSON OF MISSED MEETING

___UR___

H O M E   R E A L T Y

_____
_____   ⟵ _Date and_
_____   _address_
_____

Dear _____ :

You were missed at the [training session on Wednesday, April 1, as well as the office meeting and property caravan on Wednesday, April 8]. If you have any difficulties, I would be happy to provide any advice or assistance that I can offer.

Our office works as a team, and we try to help each other. We also view training and office meetings as important functions to aid all personnel.

It is important that every team member share his or her knowledge, experience, and support with others. I look forward to your attendance and support in the future.

Sincerely,

_____

NOTE: _Whenever possible, handle personnel matters in person rather than by letter._

Do not demand that the salesperson attend meetings, as this could be evidence that the salesperson is an employee rather than an independent contractor.

NOTICE TO SALESPERSON—UNAUTHORIZED ABSENCE

UR
H O M E   R E A L T Y

_____
_____   ← *Date and*
_____   *address*
_____

Dear _____:

On [Wednesday, March 1], you were scheduled for [1. floor time 2. an open house at (111 Circle Drive)]. You were not present, and because I was not notified you would be absent, no other arrangements could be made.

When a salesperson misses [1. floor time, we have inadequate coverage, which results in wasted advertising dollars and lost opportunities 2. an open house, not only do we waste advertising dollars, the potential is there to not only upset owners, but buyers as well who have made a trip to see a home that is not open].

Although I realize there are legitimate emergencies, nevertheless it is imperative that the office be notified as soon as possible of any absence when you are scheduled to be present.

Sincerely,

_____

NOTE: *A personal meeting is the preferred way to handle a matter such as this.*

PROBLEM NOTIFICATION

UR
HOME REALTY

————————————
————————————   ← *Date and*
————————————   *address*
————————————

Dear ————————————:

I am sorry to say that I have received a complaint alleging [that you informed the buyer of 2101 Clement Avenue (Donald Riley) that the house was connected to city sewer when it was served by a septic system].

[1. Could you please meet with me 2. Could you please meet with our attorney and me] on [Friday, April 12, at 4 P.M.] at [5 Crescent Boulevard, Suite 1800]?

[1. I have arranged a meeting between (Mr. Riley, you, and me) at (our office) at (4 P.M. on Thursday, April 12). 2. If you could come at (3 P.M.), it will give me a chance to get all the facts straight.]

Yours truly,

————————————

COMMISSION DISPUTE BETWEEN AGENTS

UR
H O M E   R E A L T Y

_____

_____ ← *Date and*
                    address

_____

_____

Dear _____:

I would like to meet with you and [Charles] in my office on [April 1], at [4 P.M.], to resolve the disagreement over the entitlement to the [1. listing 2. sales] commission for the [1. listing of 2. sale of] [111 West Jackson Street].

Sincerely,

_____

OFFICE DISPUTE DECISION

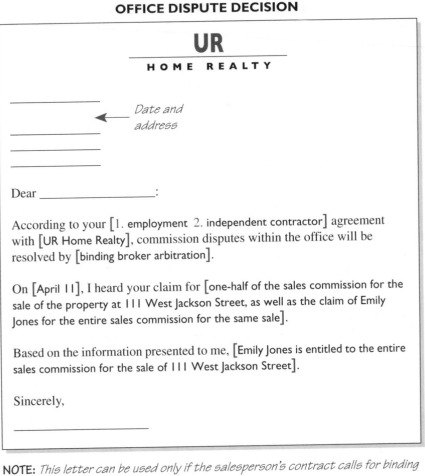

UR

H O M E   R E A L T Y

⟵ *Date and address*

Dear _____:

According to your [1. employment 2. independent contractor] agreement with [UR Home Realty], commission disputes within the office will be resolved by [binding broker arbitration].

On [April 11], I heard your claim for [one-half of the sales commission for the sale of the property at 111 West Jackson Street, as well as the claim of Emily Jones for the entire sales commission for the same sale].

Based on the information presented to me, [Emily Jones is entitled to the entire sales commission for the sale of 111 West Jackson Street].

Sincerely,

_____

NOTE: *This letter can be used only if the salesperson's contract calls for binding arbitration by the broker.*

The preferred approach would be to notify the parties in person of your decision.

SALESPERSON ACHIEVEMENT—CONGRATULATIONS

UR
H O M E   R E A L T Y

← *Date and address*

Dear _____:

Congratulations on [1. your first sale over ($1,000,000) 2. your first exchange 3. exceeding your sales goal for (February) 4. being the top (1. selling 2. listing) salesperson in our office for the month of (February)]!

I hope this accomplishment is merely a prelude to even greater achievements. Use this as just one stepping stone to the future.

Warmest regards,

_____

SPECIAL RECOGNITION—TRAINING COMPLETION
OR PROFESSIONAL DESIGNATION

UR
H O M E   R E A L T Y

_____
_____ ← _Date and_
_____   _address_
_____

Dear _____:

You may be justifiably proud of your accomplishments in [1. completing the Certified Residential Specialist (CRS) program   2. attaining the professional designation of Graduate of the REALTORS® Institute (GRI)]. I know that it wasn't easy, but I am sure the feeling of confidence, prestige within the industry, and, most importantly, the ability to better serve buyers and sellers makes the time well spent.

Congratulations—not just from me, but from our entire profession!

Sincerely,

_____

[P.S. Enclosed is a press release that will inform our community of your accomplishment.]

SALESPERSON AWARD

UR
H O M E   R E A L T Y

_____
← — *Date and*
_____   *address*
_____
_____

Dear _____:

This is to inform you that you are the grand winner of [salesperson of the month for January]. This award was achieved with [your sales of $3,851,000].

You can claim the award of [a three-day Las Vegas holiday for two] at [Anderson Travel].

Our warmest congratulations,

_____

[P.S. Enclosed is a copy of the press release we issued about your accomplishment.]

NOTE: *Awards should generally be made before the entire sales force. If a notice is used, the notice should be by telegram, express carrier service, or special delivery letter to emphasize the importance of the achievement.*

HAPPY BIRTHDAY #1

UR

H O M E   R E A L T Y

_____

_____   ← _Date and_
                        address

_____

_____

Dear _____:

Well, another year has passed. In retrospect, it has been a good year for you. Your fellow workers respect you as a knowledgeable and caring person. You are dedicated and have taken the reins of your own destiny. Most important, we regard you as our friend.

A very Happy Birthday, [Martin], from all of us!

_____   _____

_____   _____

_____   _____

NOTE: _A letter is a warmer approach than just a card. A small gift such as a quality pen might be appropriate._

HAPPY BIRTHDAY #2

Happy Birthday, [Clarence]!

We all wish you the very best on your birthday:

Good Health

Good Friends

[Happy Family]

Prosperity

We hope you are with us at [UR Home Realty] to celebrate a great many more of them. Again—a very Happy Birthday!

NOTE: *The entire staff should sign. The card could be attached to a metallic helium balloon anchored on the agent's desk with a box of candy or other small gift.*

WEDDING ANNIVERSARY

UR
H O M E   R E A L T Y

_____
_____   ⟵ *Date and*
_____   *address*
_____

Dear _____ :

My very best wishes to both of you on your wedding anniversary! As a small token of my personal regard for you, I have enclosed [a certificate for dinner for two at the Golden Palm].

It is my sincere hope that you have a joyful celebration of this and many more anniversaries.

Very sincerely,

_____

NOTE: *Include both the husband's and wife's names in the salutation.*

ANNIVERSARY WITH FIRM

UR
H O M E   R E A L T Y

← *Date and address*

Dear _____:

I don't know if you noticed, but it's our anniversary. On [June 1], it will have been [five] years since you joined [UR Home Realty]. These years have been filled with many successes and a lot of hard work. During this time, you have helped to make possible the dream of home ownership for many families.

I want you to realize that your efforts have not gone unnoticed or unappreciated. I am proud to have you with the firm and look forward to a great many more anniversaries.

Congratulations!

Very sincerely,

_____

BIRTH OF SON OR DAUGHTER

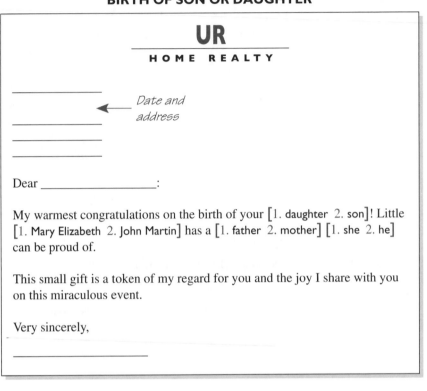

UR
H O M E   R E A L T Y

⟵ *Date and*
address

Dear _____:

My warmest congratulations on the birth of your [1. daughter 2. son]! Little [1. Mary Elizabeth 2. John Martin] has a [1. father 2. mother] [1. she 2. he] can be proud of.

This small gift is a token of my regard for you and the joy I share with you on this miraculous event.

Very sincerely,

_____

DEATH IN AGENT'S FAMILY

_____
UR
H O M E   R E A L T Y

_____
_____   ← *Date and address*
_____
_____

Dear _____:

Please accept my sincere condolences to you [and your son] on your recent loss. I know how much you thought of [Mary Jane] and can understand your feelings at this time.

[Mary Jane] brought joy to the lives of [her] family and friends, and [her] memory will live on in those whose lives [she] influenced.

[According to your wishes, I have made a donation to (The American Cancer Society) in (Mary Jane's) name.]

Thinking of you,

_____

NOTE: *This personal note is sent in addition to any flowers you may have sent for the funeral.*

DEATH OF SALESPERSON OR ASSOCIATE

UR
H O M E   R E A L T Y

_____
_____   ⟵ *Date and*
_____   *address*
_____

Dear _____:

I wish to offer my personal condolences to you. [Mary] was [1. an associate broker 2. a salesperson] with [UR Home Realty] for [1. (seven) years 2. all too short a time]. [She] was liked and respected by all of us as well as by the many clients whose real estate needs [she] helped to meet. [Mary] gave unsparingly of [herself] in helping others.

I share in your feeling of loss and want you to know that [Mary] will be truly missed.

[According to your wishes], I have made a donation to [1. The American Cancer Society 2. The Multiple Sclerosis Society] in [Mary's] name.

Yours truly,

_____

NOTE: *This letter would be sent to a spouse or parent upon the death of an agent.*

AGENT WHO VOLUNTARILY LEFT OFFICE

UR

H O M E   R E A L T Y

_____
_____ ◄— *Date and*
                    address
_____

_____

Dear _____:

I would like to take this opportunity to thank you for your professional efforts with [UR Home Realty] over the past [five years].

I wish you [1. happiness 2. success] for your future. [I want you to know that you will always have a home with (UR Home Realty).]

[Of course, you will promptly receive all commissions upon closing of transactions, in accord with our agreement.]

[We would appreciate if you would return (office keys, signs, and so on) to us as soon as practical.]

[If in the future you need a recommendation, do not hesitate to contact me.]

Sincerely,

_____

Enclosure: ◄— *Card*

NOTE: *This letter will help to keep your relationship open with an employee who may have left for perceived "greener pastures." It will also aid in future agent cooperation if the agent joins a competing firm.*

LETTER OF RECOMMENDATION

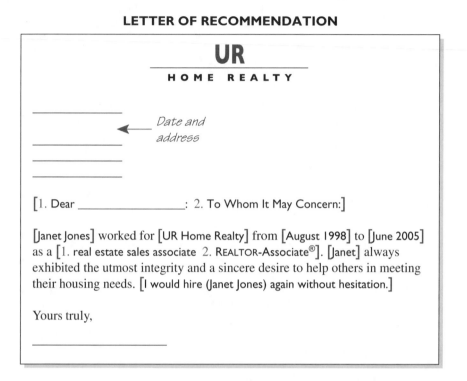

UR

H O M E   R E A L T Y

_____

⟵ *Date and*
_____   *address*

_____

_____

[1. Dear _____: 2. To Whom It May Concern:]

[Janet Jones] worked for [UR Home Realty] from [August 1998] to [June 2005] as a [1. real estate sales associate 2. REALTOR-Associate®]. [Janet] always exhibited the utmost integrity and a sincere desire to help others in meeting their housing needs. [I would hire (Janet Jones) again without hesitation.]

Yours truly,

_____

NOTICE TO SALESPERSON—TERMINATION

UR
H O M E   R E A L T Y

_____
_____ ← *Date and*
                  address
_____
_____

Dear _____ :

I am very sorry to inform you that we are unable to retain your services as a [1. sales associate 2. REALTOR-Associate®] with [UR Home Realty]. [1. I have enclosed your real estate license. 2. Our office will strictly honor your contract rights for sales and listings in progress. 3. Please drop off your office keys and return all (signs and lockboxes) as soon as possible.]

I wish you every success in your future endeavors, and if I can be of any help to you or if you have any questions, please contact me personally.

Sincerely,

_____

NOTE: *Normally, you should handle this in a face-to-face meeting. Avoid criticism or any accusations of dishonesty, because either could later be construed as libel.*

CHAPTER

PRESS RELEASES

TRANSMITTAL LETTER—PRESS RELEASE

UR
H O M E   R E A L T Y

Date and
address

Dear _____:

Enclosed is a press release [as well as a photograph with caption] concerning [Mr. Frederick Schmidt, who has recently been awarded the Certified Residential Specialist designation].

[We believe this significant achievement deserves community recognition.]

If you have any questions or desire further information, please contact me.

Yours truly,

_____

Enclosures: ◄—— _Card, photo, and press release_

NOTE: _Use masking tape as a hinge on the back of the photo so that the caption can be read below the high-contrast, black and white, glossy 5 x 7. Be certain to identify persons shown._

NEW OWNER

[Retired Banker Chooses Meadowbrook]

Mr. and Mrs. [Angus McCook] have recently purchased [a new home on Clancy Lane in Meadowbrook]. [Mr. McCook was active in banking for 40 years, having started as a teller with the Midvale Bank and rising to the presidency of the Newport Banking Group, one of the largest bank holding companies in the state.]

[Mr. and Mrs. McCook] indicated that they were attracted to [Meadowbrook] because of [1. the choice of several outstanding golf courses 2. its general country atmosphere 3. its proximity to the amenities of urban life]. The purchase was arranged through the [Meadowbrook office of UR Home Realty].

Enclosure: ◄— *Photo*

NOTE: *A press release about a buyer is appropriate when the buyer has a distinguished or interesting background. Photos with captions should be included. Consider a photo of the buyer(s) in front of the property showing a sold sign. Always obtain the buyer's permission before publicizing a purchase.*

SALE AND PURCHASE

[Smith Building Sold]

[Jim Anderson] of [UR Home Realty] recently sold [the Smith Building] at [5 Commercial Avenue]. The former owners, [Alice and Gertrude Smith], owned this landmark property for [45] years.

The purchasers, [Mr. and Mrs. Thomas Blake] of [San Juno], have indicated that they will [1. extensively remodel the property 2. move their offices to the property]. [Mr. Blake is president of Blake Motors in Covina.]

[This sale brings the first quarter sales of (UR Home Realty) to over ($27 million), which is an increase of (16) percent from last year's sales. (Mr. Joseph Lane, vice president of sales,) has indicated that interest in large commercial properties such as the Smith Building has increased significantly and he predicts continued sales increases in the foreseeable future.]

Enclosure: ◄—— *Photo*

NOTE: *If a building is well known or has historical significance, a press release would be appropriate when it is listed for sale or sold.*

Include a captioned photo of the property, possibly with the buyers and the agent in front of the property.

Always obtain permission of both buyer and seller to publicize a sale.

GROUNDBREAKING

New Project—[Woodlake Village]

[Wilson Developers] held their official groundbreaking for the new [122 single-family home Woodlake Village development] on [Wednesday, March 1]. Located [on the northwest corner of Dunn Road and Woodlake Parkway], the [three- and four-bedroom family homes] will feature [1. up to (2,400) square feet 2. three-car garages, tile roofs, and Eurostyle kitchens].

[Peggy Johnson,] project sales coordinator for [UR Home Realty] and the exclusive sales agent for [Woodlake Village], has indicated that the choice location coupled with moderate prices, starting at [$295,500] with [6 percent] financing, has already created an exceptional word-of-mouth interest in the development. According to [Peggy Johnson], the early reservations have been primarily from [1. professionals in the real estate and construction industries 2. telecom professionals].

Enclosure: ◀── *Photo*

NOTE: *For groundbreaking ceremonies, consider including a captioned photograph with local civic leaders and a builder representative as well as an agent of your firm. An artist's rendering of a model home would also be appropriate.*

SUBDIVISION OPENING

Grand Opening—[Woodlake Village]

The grand opening of [Wilson Development's] new [Woodlake Village] is scheduled for [Saturday and Sunday, June 5 and 6]. Located [on the northwest corner of Dunn Road and Woodlake Parkway], the development features [three- and four-bedroom family homes starting at $329,000, with 6½ percent financing available]. All homes include [three-car garages, tile roofs, and Euro-style kitchens].

[Peggy Johnson,] the [sales coordinator] for [UR Home Realty], which is the exclusive sales agent for the project, has indicated that exceptional interest has developed in [Woodlake Village] due to [its choice location and the moderate pricing policy].

According to [Ms. Johnson], the grand opening will feature [six decorator-furnished models, and there will be refreshments and gifts for opening-day visitors].

Enclosure: ◄—— *Photo*

NOTE: *You should include a photo or artist's rendering of one of the models. Placing ads on the opening generally ensures publication of your press release.*

FIRST SALE IN SUBDIVISION

First Sale Made at [English Village]

[UR Home Realty], the exclusive sales agent for [English Village], has announced that [Dr. and Mrs. Timothy Marks] are the first home purchasers in [the exclusive enclave of 16 estate homes in Bellwood]. [Dr. Marks is a pediatrician and is on the staff of Mercy Hospital.]

The [Marks] chose a [3,600 square-foot English country design]. According to [Mrs. Marks], they decided on [English Village] because of [the huge lots, scenic views, quality design and construction, as well as the country ambience, which is so important with four small children].

[Currently, three of the estate homes are under construction with the Marks's home scheduled for completion by August 15.]

Enclosure: ◄—— *Photo*

NOTE: *For a press release that provides information about a buyer, be certain to obtain permission from the buyer. A captioned picture of the purchasing family standing in front of the home, even if the home is not completed, would be appropriate.*

In addition to publicity about your firm, a press release such as this one significantly reduces the possibility that the buyer will attempt to avoid the purchase closing.

MILESTONE SALE IN SUBDIVISION

[(100th) Sale Announced for Orchard Heights]

[Henry Ammenson], [project director] for [UR Home Realty], has announced that the [100th new home in Orchard Heights has been sold since November]. According to [Mr. Ammenson], this subdivision has been one of the most successful in the area because of the tremendous value offered in housing at a premier location. The problem has been not being able to build the homes fast enough. [Mr. Ammenson indicates that, at the present sales rate, the entire subdivision will be sold out by June 1.]

Enclosure: ◀—— Photo

NOTE: Consider a captioned photograph of the buying family in front of their new home. Never send a press release out about a transaction, buyer, or seller without written permission from the people involved.

OFFICE OPENING OR RELOCATION

[1. **UR Home Realty Opens Newhall Office**
2. **UR Home Realty Expands**]

[UR Home Realty] has announced [1. the opening of a (second) office (in the Murray Building at 136 West 31st Street in Lynnwood) 2. the relocation of its (Lynnwood) office to the (Murray Building at 136 West 31st Street)].

According to [Thomas Johnson, President of UR Home Realty], the [1. expansion 2. move] was necessary to better meet the needs of [Lynnwood] residents.

Although the office will specialize in [residential sales], its services will also include [investment sales and property management]. [The new office will also coordinate the sales of several new subdivisions in the area.] [UR Home Realty] currently has [more than 60 salespeople with total sales last year exceeding $500 million, making this firm one of the fastest-growing brokerage offices in the county]!

Enclosure: ◄——— *Photo*

NOTE: *Consider a captioned photograph of the entire office staff in front of the new office or with a For Sale sign.*

NEW ASSOCIATE OR SALESPERSON

[Henry Gibbs] Joins [UR Home Realty]

[Thomas Flynn], [General Manager] of [UR Home Realty], announced that [Mr. Henry Gibbs] recently joined the firm as [1. a sales associate 2. a REALTOR-Associate® 3. an associate broker]. [Mr. Gibbs] will be involved with [home sales, primarily in the West Valley].

[Mr. Gibbs] is [a graduate of Syracuse University and has spent 12 years as a food broker in Chicago]. [He] obtained [his] real estate license [two years ago, and he was previously associated with Boniface Construction Company, selling new homes in the Bellwood Heights development]. [Mr. Gibbs is a member of Thunderbird Country Club and resides in Bellwood Heights with his wife Eileen and their two daughters.]

Enclosure: ◀—— *Photo*

NOTE: *Send a captioned photo with all personnel press releases.*

PROMOTION OR APPOINTMENT

New [Sales Manager]

[Henry Clyde, President of UR Home Realty,] has announced that [Jane Jones] has been appointed [sales manager] of [UR Home Realty]. [Ms. Jones] brings a wealth of experience to the position. [She] was formerly associated with [Smith Realty] as [assistant sales manager]. [Ms. Jones has had over (eight)] years of experience in [1. sales 2. real estate sales]. [Ms. Jones] has been with [UR Home Realty] for [four years]. [Ms. Jones has received numerous honors, including membership in the prestigious UR Home Realty Ten Million Dollar Roundtable.]

[1. Ms. Jones received her bachelor's degree in business from Yale University. 2. Ms. Jones attended New York University.] [She] lives with [her] family in [Midvale Heights]. [She has two children, John, nine years old, and Tammy, six.] [Her husband Clarence teaches English at South High School.] [Ms. Jones] is active in [Soroptimists and is an assistant Girl Scout leader].

Enclosure: ◀—— *Photo*

NOTE: *Consider a captioned photo of a broker with the new [sales manager] either in front of the office or near an office sign. If the person did not graduate from a school, you can use "attended." If she or he graduated, indicate "graduated from" or the degree received.*

PROFESSIONAL DESIGNATION

[Chris Jones Earns Professional Designation]

[Chris Jones], a[n] [1. sales associate 2. associate broker 3. REALTOR-Associate®] with [UR Home Realty], has recently earned the coveted [Certified Residential Specialist (CRS)] designation. This [is the highest] professional award of the [Residential Sales Council] and is awarded only after a [1. REALTOR® 2. real estate professional] has met [high standards for experience and has also completed a rigorous course of training]. [Mr. Jones] is now one of just a few real estate professionals in [our community] who may use [CRS] after [his] name.

[Mr. Jones has been a real estate professional for 17 years. He is a graduate of Notre Dame, where he earned his degree in marketing. He lives in Westwood with his wife, Ellen, and their two daughters. Mr. Jones is active in the Rotary Club and is a deacon at Westwood Community Church.]

Enclosure: ◄──── *Photo*

SALES AWARD

Salesperson of the [1. **Month** 2. **Year**]

[Joseph Evans], [Sales Manager] of [UR Home Realty], has announced that [Patricia Jones] has been named [sales associate] of the [1. month 2. year].

During [1. March 2. the past year], [Ms. Jones] has [1. sold 2. listed] [1. more than $6 million in real estate 2. 19 properties]. [Ms. Jones] has been associated with [UR Home Realty] [1. since 1993 2. for seven years]. Before joining [UR Home Realty], [she] was [a professor of zoology at Western State University]. [Ms. Jones lives in Middletown with her husband and four children.]

Enclosure: ◄——— *Photo*

NOTE: *Enclose a photo of a broker and the salesperson receiving an award.*

SALE OF REAL ESTATE FIRM

New Owner Announced for [UR Home Realty]

[UR Home Realty] has announced that the firm has been sold [by its founder, Angus Johnson, to the firm's General Manager, Thomas Flynn. Angus Johnson founded UR Home Realty in 1947, and it has been the oldest real estate firm in the county under the same ownership.]

[UR Home Realty] currently has [62 salespeople operating from their offices at 922 West Broadway]. [Angus Johnson] estimates that since it was founded, the firm has sold over [25,000] properties, with total sales [in the hundreds of millions of dollars].

[Thomas Flynn has been associated with UR Home Realty for 11 years, starting as a salesperson, and has served the last four years as General Manager. Mr. Flynn, who is a business graduate of Michigan State University, indicates that the firm's name, as well as the philosophy and policies of Angus Johnson, will continue.]

Enclosure: ◄—— *Photo*

NOTE: *Include a photograph showing both former owner (if possible) and successor.*

MISCELLANEOUS LETTERS

LETTER TO NEWSPAPER ABOUT AD COPY—
TRANSMITTAL

UR
H O M E   R E A L T Y

_____
          ◄——— *Date and*
_____   *address*

_____

_____

Dear _____:

I wish to run the following ads ⌈1. from (Sunday, April 3) through (Saturday, April 9) 2. on (Sunday, April 3)⌉ in the classified section under the following categories:

Category: _____

_____

_____

_____

Category: _____

_____

_____

_____

Please bill these ads to our account.

Yours truly,

_____

Enclosure: ◄——— *Card*

NOTE: *Give any instructions about size or style of type, if applicable.*

NOTICE TO NEWSPAPER OF MISTAKE IN ADVERTISEMENT

UR
H O M E   R E A L T Y

_____

_____   ← *Date and*
                        address
_____

_____

Attention: Classified Advertisement Department Editor

[1. Dear Editor: 2. To Whom It May Concern:]

On [September 10] we placed an ad under the category [Real Estate] to run on [Sunday, September 16].

The ad was to read as follows: _____

_____

_____

Due to your error, the ad appeared on [September 17] on page [37], [under the category (Appliances)], [and read as follows]: _____

_____

_____

Because of the error, [1. the effectiveness of the ad was materially diminished 2. the ad was of no benefit to our firm]. We therefore expect [1. an appropriate adjustment because of your error 2. the ad charge to be fully credited on our next billing 3. the ad to be run on (October 12) without charge].

Yours truly,

_____

Enclosures: ← *Card, ad copy*

NOTE: *You may wish to use a yellow highlighter to indicate an error in the ad copy or placement.*

CHARITY TICKET RESPONSE

_____**UR**_____

H O M E   R E A L T Y

_____

_____   ← *Date and*
                             address
_____

_____

Dear _____ :

Enclosed is our check for [$30] for [two] tickets. The remaining tickets are enclosed.

We are always happy to provide assistance to local organizations. We wish you good luck on your event.

Yours truly,

_____

Enclosures: ◄─── *Card, check, tickets*

NOTE: *Charities generally send out books of tickets. This response allows you to be positive without purchasing all of the tickets.*

CHRISTMAS CARD CAPTION

May the joyous holiday spirit
extend throughout the coming year.

Wishing you and yours a very special

Season's Greetings

from all of us at
[UR Home Realty]!

NOTE: *This short season's greetings would be appropriate with a photograph of your staff and families and/or with the personal signatures of your staff.*

INDEX OF LETTERS

C D - R O M   G U I D E

To Install the Application

- Insert the CD-ROM into the CD-ROM drive; the program should automatically begin the installation process.

- If the installation does not automatically begin, click "Start" and then "Run."

- In the "Run" window, use the "Browse" button to navigate to the CD-ROM drive and select the setup.exe file.

- Follow the installation prompts.

How to Use This Application

The forms processing application provides a minimized word processor to allow you to customize, revise, and change the forms and letters contained on this disc. We've provided it to allow you to be productive immediately with the forms and/or letters contained in this guide. To open the application from Program Manager or the Start menu, select the Dearborn program group and click on the icon. You can also start the program using the shortcut on your desktop. The basic commands and features of the application are described below.

To Select a Form to Edit

Select the **File** and **Open Form** command to access the forms available with this application. The Open Form command presents the forms dialog box where you can select a form to customize. To select a form, click on a title in the list on the left side of the dialog box. The form title and a brief description of the form appear on the right side of the dialog box. If this is the form you want to edit, select **Open.**

Editing the Form

To edit the form and customize it for your use, select the Find button in the tool-bar at the top of the form window to automatically locate fields in the form where you need to enter information. These fields are noted with a ">". Of course, you may change or revise any of the text in the form at will.

The menu at the top of the form provides you with several controls. These are as follows:

- **Edit:** You can cut, copy, and paste segments of text.

- **Style:** you can bold, italicize, and underline text, as well as select a font and type size for selected text.

Many of the functions available as menu selections are also available as button commands in the toolbar. These are:

- **Font:** Select from the fonts available on your system by pressing the down arrow and clicking on the font name.

- **Size:** Select the font size by clicking the down arrow and highlighting the font size.

- **Bold (B), Italic (I), Underline (U):** Select the text you want to change and press the button to change the format.

- **Justification:** You may change the text to flush right, left, centered, or justi-fied by selecting the text and pressing the appropriate button.

Note: Save any edited forms under a different or new file name.

Favorites

If you are like most people, you'll likely use a few forms repeatedly. This appli-cation allows you to save forms as "favorites" to provide quick access to those forms frequently used. **To add a form to Favorites:**

- Open a form as you normally would.

- Choose **Favorites** from the File menu and select **Add to Favorites.**

- Enter the name for the file and choose Save. (The file will be saved in a default directory called RE_FAVS.)

- To reselect the form, select favorites from the menu, and select Open Favor-ite Files. Select the file and press Open.

Help

To learn more about the forms application and the commands available to you, select **Help** from the menu.

If You Already Have a Word Processor . . .

If you have and are already familiar with one or more of the word processing applications available to you, you can use the functionality available in those programs to work with these forms. Select and edit any one of the forms directly from the forms subdirectory created on your hard drive during installation. The files are unformatted ASCII text files that work with all current applications. Text that you need to enter in order to complete a form is preceded by a ">" character. Using your word processor's search function to locate these areas will allow you to quickly customize the forms/letters to suit your needs.

Another way to use the forms in this application with other word processors is to save the file as either a text file (txt) or rich text file (rtf). To do this, select **File** and **Open** from the menu. Open the file you wish to edit and choose **Save As.** Select or enter the name of the file and choose the location where you want it to go. Select **OK.** Open the file in your word processor as you would any other file and edit. (Keep in mind that once you work on a file in another word processor and save it, it probably won't work in the forms processor application without conversion back to a standard text or ASCII file.)

Technical Support

TECHNICAL SUPPORT IS NOT AVAILABLE ON THE ENCLOSED CD-ROM. Please read the installation and operating instructions carefully before attempting to use the CD-ROM.

LICENSE AGREEMENT

OPENING ENVELOPE VOIDS RETURNABILITY OR MONEY-BACK GUARANTEE
PLEASE READ THIS DOCUMENT CAREFULLY BEFORE BREAKING THIS SEAL

By breaking this sealed envelope, you agree to become bound by the terms of this license. If you do not agree to the terms of this license do not use the software and promptly return the unopened package and textbook within thirty (30) days to the place where you obtained it for a refund.

This Software is licensed, not sold to you by DEARBORN FINANCIAL PUBLISHING, INC., owner of the product, for use only under the terms of this License, and DEARBORN FINANCIAL PUBLISHING, INC. reserves any rights not expressly granted to you.

1. **LICENSE:** This License allows you to:
    (a) Use the Software only on a single personal computer at a time, except the Software may be executed from a common disk shared by multiple CPUs provided that one authorized copy of the Software has been licensed from DEARBORN FINANCIAL PUBLIHSING, INC. for each CPU executing the Software. DEARBORN FINANCIAL PUBLISHING, INC. does not, however, guarantee that the Software will function properly in your multiple CPU, multi-user environment. The Software may not be used with any gateways, bridges, modems, and/or network extenders that allow the Software to be used on multiple CPUs unless one authorized copy of the Software has been licensed from DEARBORN FINANCIAL PUBLISHING, INC. for each CPU executing the software.
    (b) Configure the Software for your own use by adding or removing fonts, desk accessories, and/or device drivers.

2. **RESTRICTION:** You may not distribute copies of the Software to others or electronically transfer the Software from one computer to another over a network and/or zone. The Software contains trade secrets and to protect them you may not de-compile, reverse engineer, disassemble, cross assemble or otherwise change and/or reduce the Software to any other form. You may not modify, adapt, translate, rent, lease, loan, resell for profit, distribute, network, or create derivative works based upon the Software or any part thereof.

3. **TERMINATION:** This License is effective unless terminated. This License will terminate immediately without notice from DEARBORN FINANCIAL PUBLISHING, INC. if you fail to comply with any provision of this License. Upon termination you must destroy the Software and all copies thereof.

4. **EXPORT LAW ASSURANCES:** You agree that the Software will not be shipped, transferred, or exported into any country prohibited by the United States Export Administration Act and the regulations thereunder nor will be used for any purpose prohibited by the Act.

5. **LIMITED WARRANTY, DISCLAIMER, LIMITATION OF REMEDIES AND DAMAGES:** The information in this software (Materials) is sold with the understanding that the author, publisher, developer, and distributor are not engaged in rendering legal, accounting, banking, security, or other professional advice. If legal advice, accounting advice, security investment advice, bank or tax advice, or other expert professional assistance is required, the services of a competent professional with expertise in that field should be sought. These materials have been developed using ideas from experience and survey information from various research, lectures, and publications. The information contained in these materials is believed to be reliable only at the time of publication and it cannot be guaranteed as it is applied to any particular individual or situation. The author, publisher, developer, and distributor specifically disclaim any liability or risk, personal or otherwise, incurred directly or indirectly as a consequence of the use of an application of the information contained in these materials or the live lectures that could accompany their distribution. In no event will the author, publisher, developer, or distributor be liable to the purchaser for any amount greater than the purchase price of the materials.

DEARBORN FINANCIAL PUBLISHING, INC.'s warranty on the media, including any implied warranty of merchant ability or fitness for a particular purpose, is limited in duration to thirty (30) days from the date of the original retail. If a disk fails to work or if a disk becomes damaged, you may obtain a replacement disk by returning the original disk together with a brief explanation note and a dated sales receipt to:

DEARBORN FINANCIAL PUBLISHING, INC.
30 SOUTH WACKER DRIVE, SUITE 2500
CHICAGO, IL 60606-7481

The replacement warranty set forth above is the sole and exclusive remedy against DEARBORN FINANCIAL PUBLISHING, INC. for breach of warrant, express or implied or for any default whatsoever relating to condition of the software. DEARBORN FINANCIAL PUBLISHING, INC. makes no other warranties or representation, either express or implied, with respect to this software or documentation, quality, merchantability performance or fitness for a particular purpose as a result. This software is sold with only the limited warranty with respect to CD replacement as provided above, and you, the Licensee, are assuming all other risks as to its quality and performance. In no event will DEARBORN FINANCIAL PUBLISHING, INC. or its developers, directors, officers, employees, or affiliates be liable for direct, incidental, indirect, special, or consequential damages (including damages for loss of business profits, business interruption, loss of business information and the like) resulting from any defect in this software or its documentation or arising our of the use of or inability to use the software or accompanying documentation even if DEARBORN FINANCIAL PUBLISHING, INC., an authorized DEARBORN FINANCIAL PUBLISHING, INC. representative, or a DEARBORN FINANCIAL PUBLISHING, INC. affiliate has been advised of the possibility of such damage.

DEARBORN FINANCIAL PUBLISHING, INC. MAKES NO REPRESENTATION OR WARRANTY REGARDING THE RESULTS OBTAINABLE THROUGH USE OF THE SOFTWARE.

No oral or written information or advice given by DEARBORN FINANCIAL PUBLISHING, INC., its dealers, distributors, agents, affiliates, developers, officers, directors, or employees shall create a warranty or in any way increase the scope of this warranty.

Some states do not allow the exclusion or limitation of implied warranties or liabilities for incidental or consequential damages, so the above limitation or exclusion may not apply to you. This warranty gives you specific legal rights, and you may also have other rights which vary from state to state.

COPYRIGHT NOTICE: This software and accompanying manual are copyrighted with all rights reserved by DEARBORN FINANCIAL PUBLISHING, INC. Under United States copyright laws, the software and its accompanying documentation may not be copied in whole or in part except in normal use of the software or the reproduction of a backup copy for archival purposes only. Any other copying, selling, or otherwise distributing this software or manual is hereby expressly forbidden.

SIGNATURE _____
SIGN IF BEING RETURNED UNOPENED FOR REFUND